© Copyright 2022- All rights reserved.

This document is geared towards providing exact and reliable information regarding the topic and issue covered. The publication is sold with the idea that the publisher is not required to render accounting, officially permitted, or otherwise, qualified services. If advice is necessary, legal or professional, a practised individual in the profession should be ordered.

From a Declaration of Principles which was accepted and approved equally by a Committee of the American Bar Association and a Committee of Publishers and Associations.

In no way is it legal to reproduce, duplicate, or transmit any part of this document in either electronic means or printed format. Recording of this publication is strictly prohibited and any storage of this document is not allowed unless with written permission from the publisher. All rights reserved.

The information provided herein is stated to be truthful and consistent, in that any liability, in terms of inattention or otherwise, by any usage or abuse of any policies, processes, or directions contained within is the solitary and utter responsibility of the recipient reader. Under no circumstances will any legal responsibility or blame be held against the publisher for any reparation, damages, or monetary loss due to the information herein, either directly or indirectly.

Introduction

Are you looking for the most tantalising recipes to prepare for the upcoming holiday season, such as Thanksgiving or Christmas? Since we have compiled what we are calling "The Complete Christmas Cookbook for Aspiring Chefs," there is no need for you to explore any further.

This book will make it easy for you to leave an impression that will linger on your friends, loved ones, and family during the Christmas season.

We have included more than one hundred of our most treasured seasonal recipes, many of which come highly recommended by well-known chefs and culinary experts from all over the world. We've got you covered whether you want to prepare eggnog that will be remembered for a long time or a turkey roast that will take people's breath away.

Table of content

	Page
Roast Turkey with Herbal Rub	5
Herb-Roasted Turkey with Citrus Glaze	7
Turkey Breast Braised with Garlic and Rice	10
Moist Glazed Ham	11
Old Fashioned Bread Stuffing	13
Green Onion and Cornbread Stuffing	16
Cranberry Chutney	17
Gravy Secrets	18
Basic Turkey Gravy	22
Giblet Gravy	24
Guilt-Free Turkey Gravy	26
Sweet Potato Casserole	27
Mashed Sweet Potatoes	28
Roast Garlic Mashed Potatoes	29
Crockpot Scalloped Potatoes	30
Squash Casserole	31
Stuffed Acorn Squash	32
Ice Cream Pumpkin Pie	33
Pumpkin Cake Roll	34
Pumpkin and Praline Pie	36
Famous Pumpkin Nut Bread	37
Barbecued Turkey With Maple-Mustard Sauce	38
Thanksgiving Turkey	42
Five Spiced Turkey	43
Bread And Oyster Stuffing	46
Green Onion And Cornbread Stuffing	47
Pecan Pumpkin Pie	48
Thanksgiving Cranberry Relish	49
Easy Pumpkin Cake	50
Thanksgiving Muffins	52
Thanksgiving Ambrosia	54
Thanksgiving Pumpkin Bread	55
Cranberry Sauce	57
Garlic Mashed Potatoes	58
Holiday Turkey with Michigan Maple Glaze and Cranberry Bourbon Relish	59
Cranberry Bourbon Relish	61

	Page
Apricot Honey Ham Glaze	62
Glazed Baked Ham	63
Best Pickled Eggs	64
Buttermilk Corn Fritters	66
Cheese Ball	67
Cheese Fondue	68
Cheeseball II	69
Corn Fritters	70
Creamy Cheddar Cheese Soup	71
Deviled Eggs	73
Pickled Pumpkin	74
Frosted Pecan Bites	75
Fruit Dip	76
Mini Sweet Potato Pies	77
Pumpkin Dip	80
Roasted Pumpkin Seeds	81
Sausage Balls	82
Seasoned Crackers	83
Spiced Pumpkin Dip	84
Stuffed Jalapenos	85
Stuffed Mushrooms II	86
Sugar Coated Pecans	88
Sweet Pickled Eggs	89
Sweet Potato Balls	90
Tasty Toothpick Appetizers	91
Thanksgiving Cheese Ball	92
Thanksgiving Won-Tons	94
Turkey Dumplings	95
Vegetable Dip	96
Apple Orchard Punch	97
Apple Pie	98
Cherry Cider	99
Coffee Liqueur	100
Cranberry Pineapple Juice	101
Cranberry Punch	102
Cranberry Tea	103
Eggnog Extreme	104

	Page
Eggnog I	105
Eggnog II	106
Holiday Punch I	107
Hot Buttered Rum Batter	108
Pumpkin Pie Smoothie	109
Warm and Spicy Autumn Punch	110
Brown Bread	111
Banana Cranberry Bread	112
Best Ever Banana Bread	114
Country Banana Bread	115
Cranberry Muffins	116
Cranberry Nut Bread I	118
Cranberry Nut Bread II	118
Date and Nut Bread	120
Grandmother's Famous Cranberry Bread	121
Knodel	122
Apple Cranberry Pie	124
Cranberry Apple Pie I	125
Cranberry Apple Pie II	126
Cranberry Pecan Pie	128
Cranberry Pie I	129
Honey Baked Apples	130
Mincemeat II	131
Baked Ziti with Turkey Meatballs	132
Cranberry Stuffed Turkey Breasts	135
Pumpkin Stew	138
Savoury Pumpkin Soup	140
Spiced Turkey Roast	142
Spicy Spaghetti Squash	144
Stuffed Pumpkin I	146
Apple Strudel II	148
Bread Pudding I	150
Cherry Delight	152
Cherry Fluff	153
Chocolate Bar Fondue	154
Country Banana Bread	155
Corn Pudding II	156
Apple Cranberry Streusel Pie	157

Roast Turkey with Herbal Rub

9 servings 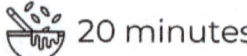 20 minutes  150 minutes

Ingredients

- 1 13-Pound WHOLE TURKEY fresh or thawed
- 1 Medium onion quartered
- 1 lemon quartered
- 1/4 Cup vegetable oil
- 1 Teaspoon dried thyme
- 1 Teaspoon dried tarragon
- 1 Tablespoon dried rosemary
- 1 Teaspoon salt
- 1/2 Teaspoon freshly ground black pepper

Preparation

- Turn on the oven to 325 degrees.
- Turkey broth can be made by saving the turkey's neck and giblets.
- Use cold running water to thoroughly wash the turkey, and then pat it dry with paper towels. Stuff the neck and body with onion and lemon quarters.
- Combine oil, seasonings, and herbs in a small bowl. Avoid ripping the skin off with your fingers when you loosen it from the breast.
- Apply the herbal mixture subcutaneously (under the skin) using a spoonful and then replace the skin
- Herb combination should be used to stuff birds and rubbed on the fowl's exterior.

Roast Turkey with Herbal Rub

🍴 9 servings 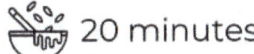 20 minutes  150 minutes

Preparation

- Skewers should be used to fasten the skin of the neck to the back. Turkeys are folded with their wings tucked under their backs. Get your legs tucked under you. All the work up to this stage can be stored in the fridge for a few hours if covered.
- The turkey should be roasted breast-side up on a rack in a big shallow (no more than 2-1/2 inches deep) roasting pan. Carefully place an oven-safe thermometer into the meatiest area of the thigh, making sure not to let it touch the bone.
- Tent the bird with foil and seal it loosely. Put the turkey in an oven that has been preheated to 325 degrees Fahrenheit for about 2.5 hours.
- Take the foil off, and use the pan juices to baste the bird. Keep roasting for another hour, or until an internal meat thermometer reads 180 degrees F.
- Take the turkey out of the oven and let it sit for about 20 minutes before you cut into it. Serve with gravy on a big plate.

Herb-Roasted Turkey with Citrus Glaze

6 servings 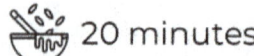 20 minutes  240 minutes

Ingredients

- 1 15-Pound WHOLE TURKEY fresh or frozen (thawed)
- 3 Large lemons
- 2 Large limes
- 1-1/2 Teaspoon salt, divided
- 1/2 Teaspoon black pepper coarsely ground
- 1/4 Cup dry white wine (see note)
- 1/4 Cup packed brown sugar
- Pan Gravy
- 1 Bunch, each fresh sage, marjoram, and thyme, divided

Preparation

- Take off the turkey's neck and giblets and save them for gravy.
- Drain the turkey carefully after rinsing it under cool running water. Use paper towels to thoroughly dry.
- For "rose" garnishes, use lemon and lime peels instead of the fruit's rind. Put in the freezer or fridge for later.
- Squeeze the lemons and limes until you have 2 teaspoons of juice from each. You may stuff the turkey with the remaining lemons and limes by slicing them in half and placing them inside. Fill the cavity with salt.
- Combine the wine, brown sugar, and citrus juices in a small bowl and set aside for the glaze.
- Carefully slip 1 tablespoon of fresh sage and 1 tablespoon of fresh marjoram under the skin of the turkey breast, taking care not to completely separate the skin. Change the covering.

Herb-Roasted Turkey with Citrus Glaze

6 servings  20 minutes  240 minutes

Preparation

- Roll the skin of the neck over and skewer it in place behind the animal's back. Pinch the turkey's wings behind its back.
- Tuck your legs back under again. Put the turkey in a large, shallow (approximately 2-1/2 inches deep), roasting pan with the breast side up on a rack.
- Season the turkey with salt, pepper, and 2 to 3 tablespoons of salad oil and rub it all over.
- Carefully place the pointed end of an oven-safe meat thermometer into the thickest portion of the thigh, making sure the thermometer doesn't touch the bone.
- For around 3 and a half hours in an oven preheated to 325 degrees Fahrenheit, roast the turkey. Baste with the drippings from the pan in the final hour of roasting. In the final 30 minutes, baste with the citrus glaze.
- Cover with a sheet of lightweight foil and leave it loose to prevent over-browning.
- The internal temperature of the thigh should reach 180 degrees F, while that of the breast should reach 170 degrees F.

Herb-Roasted Turkey with Citrus Glaze

6 servings 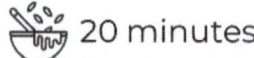 20 minutes  240 minutes

Preparation

- Take the turkey out of the oven and let it rest for at least 20 minutes before you start slicing it.
- Arrange on a large heated dish, then top with the remaining herbs and lemon and lime roses.
- To make lemon and lime roses, you'll need to peel off a continuous thin 1-inch strip of peel using a tiny sharp knife or a vegetable peeler.
- The white pith should not be cut through.
- Roll up tightly with the skin facing inward and use toothpicks to keep it closed.
- Put in a bowl of ice water and set aside until ready to serve.

Turkey Breast Braised with Garlic and Rice

🍴 6 servings 🥣 20 minutes 🍲 240 minutes

Ingredients

- 1 Cup long-grain rice
- 1 Can (14-1/2 ounces) chicken broth
- 1/2 Cup white wine
- 2 Teaspoons dried parsley
- 1/2 Teaspoon each dried rosemary, thyme and sage
- 1 Bay leaf
- 1 BONE-IN TURKEY BREAST (5-6 pounds)
- Paprika
- 3 Cloves garlic

Preparation

- Get the oven ready at 350 degrees. Mix rice, broth, wine, parsley, rosemary, thyme, sage, and bay leaf in a 5-quart Dutch oven.
- Arrange the turkey on top of the rice and season it heavily with paprika. Garlic cloves should have their stems trimmed.
- In a bowl of rice, surround the turkey with whole garlic bulbs, cut side up. Wrap foil around the top of the Dutch oven.
- Put in the oven and set the temperature to 350 degrees F.
- Until a meat thermometer placed into the thickest portion of the breast reads 170-175 degrees F, which should take around 2-1/2 to 3 hours. Stand for at least 10 minutes, preferably 15 minutes, before serving.

Moist Glazed Ham

🍴 6 servings   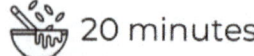 20 minutes    240 minutes

Ingredients

- Large whole ham
- 1 pound of brown sugar
- Can of Classic Coke

Preparation

- Have a 400-degree oven ready. The fat of a large whole ham should be scored in the typical diamond pattern after the rine has been removed. Use a lot of whole cloves and a big roasting pan to cook it.
- Stuff as much brown sugar as you can fit into the space atop the ham, preferably 1 pound.
- The missing piece will be left in the pan and incorporated into the glaze.
- Cook for 30–40 minutes at 400°F, or until the brown sugar melts.
- Then, very slowly, without disturbing the melting sugar, pour an entire can of Classic Coke over the ham. Turn the temperature down to 325 degrees.

Moist Glazed Ham

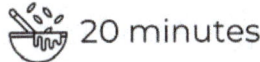 6 servings    20 minutes   240 minutes

Preparation

- Baste the meat every 30 minutes with a mixture of half burgandy wine and half pineapple juice for the remaining 4 hours.
- Also, don't forget to re-serve the juices from the pan by spooning them on top. The goal is to maintain an extremely wet environment for the duration of the cooking process.
- If you have a lot going on and are at risk of getting sidetracked, you can "tent it" with foil for the first three and a half hours. Put up the extra effort, since this ham will taste better than any other you've had.

Old Fashioned Bread Stuffing

 6 servings    20 minutes   30 minutes

Ingredients

- 3-4 loaves of white bread (or 5 if you like leftovers)
- water
- chicken broth
- insides of the turkey
- 2 bunches of celery
- 1 or 2 onions
- 2 TBSP butter
- 1/2 tsp. sage
- oysters (optional)
- mushrooms (option)

Preparation

- Cut the bread into small cubes (approximately 1 inch squares) and place them in 2 large bowls or pots the night before you intend to make the filling. Dry the bread out in the fridge overnight.
- The following day, when the turkey's insides have been removed, boil them in water in a 2/3 qt. sauce pan until done (approximately 20/30 minutes). Take out the insides and store them or throw them away. Set aside some of the water.
- The oven needs to be heated to 350 degrees.
- Mince the onion and celery by placing them in a food processor with some chopped onion and celery.
- Start by melting the butter (about 2–3 tablespoons) in a big saucepan.

Old Fashioned Bread Stuffing

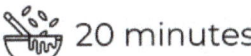 6 servings    20 minutes   45 minutes

Preparation

- Fry the onion and celery until they are hot. Stay away from the coffee! (You can also sauté mushrooms at this point if desired). You may need to saute the onion and celery in two batches if you're making a large batch of stuffing, as the amount of stuffing you make will determine how much of each you need to prepare.
- Put the sautéed onion and celery mixture on top of the stale bread.
- To the bread, onion, and celery, add half a teaspoon of sage.
- Then, drizzle the water you saved over the bread very carefully. Bread will get smaller as you do this. Careful, too much water could cause the system to overflow.
- Stuffing that turns out perfectly requires a thorough mixing and a good nose and taste.
- Chicken broth is a great liquid replacement that may be poured over bread. You may always season it up with more sage if you want it spicy.

Old Fashioned Bread Stuffing

🍴 6 servings   🥣 20 minutes   🍲 45 minutes

Preparation

- Toss in the oysters now if you're using them.
- Do not add more liquid to stuffing after it reaches a consistency where it will stay together and does not appear too dry.
- Stuff a turkey or a 913 baking dish, then bake as directed.
- Stuffing with oysters should be baked in a skillet to ensure that they are completely done.
- For 45 minutes to an hour in a preheated oven at 350 degrees, watch the oven. A golden brown crust on top of the stuffing is preferable.

Green Onion and Cornbread Stuffing

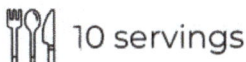 10 servings    10 minutes    45 minutes

Ingredients

- 1 Can (10-1/2 ounces) condensed French onion soup
- 1 Soup Can of water
- 1/4 Cup margarine
- 1 Cup celery cut into 1/4-inch cubes
- 1 Cup green onions thinly sliced
- 1-1/2 Teaspoons poultry seasoning
- 2 Packages (8 ounces each) of cornbread stuffing mix
- Vegetable cooking spray

Preparation

- Get the oven ready at 350 degrees.
- Put the soup, water, margarine, celery, onions, and poultry seasoning into a 5-quart saucepan and stir to combine. Bring to a boil, then turn off heat.
- Stuffing mix made from cornmeal should be added and mixed in.
- Put stuffing in a 1-1/2 quart casserole dish sprayed with vegetable cooking spray and bake.
- Cover and bake in a preheated 350°F oven for 45 minutes, or until firm.

Cranberry Chutney

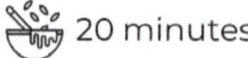 6 servings    20 minutes   25 minutes

Ingredients

- 1 Package (12 ounces) of fresh cranberries
- 1/2 Cup balsamic vinegar
- 1/2 Cup sugar
- 1 Teaspoon nutmeg
- 1 Teaspoon cinnamon
- 1 Teaspoon cayenne pepper
- 1 Teaspoon cumin

Preparation

- The cranberries, vinegar, and sugar should be brought to a boil in a medium saucepan set over high heat.
- Spices such as nutmeg, cinnamon, cayenne, and cumin can be added after the heat is lowered to a medium-low setting.
- Keep stirring constantly and simmer for 20–25 minutes, until the mixture has reached the desired thickness.

Gravy Secrets

 12 servings  5 minutes 45 minutes

Ingredients

- For each cup of gravy,
- You need one tablespoon each of fat and flour

Preparation

- Prepare a flavorful turkey broth ahead of time by boiling down the bird's bones and internal organs. Unfortunately, there will be no large, uncarved bird on the table since I like to use the bones.
- Simmer the turkey neck, heart, and gizzard with enough water to cover, along with some minced onion, celery, and 1/2 t salt, until the veggies are tender.
- The turkey liver can be diced and then simmered in the heated broth for about 15 minutes. There will be plenty of broth from the turkey bones, and you may bulk up the pan with extra veggies.

Gravy Secrets

🍴 12 servings  5 minutes 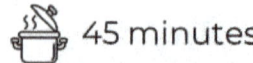 45 minutes

Preparation

- After removing the roasted turkey and roasting rack from the roasting pan, be sure to retrieve the brownings, as "that's the goodies," as Mom would say. In a glass measuring cup with a 4-cup capacity, strain the chicken fat.
- Then I use 3 tb of corn oil to scrape the bottom of the pan and remove the browned parts that have baked on. That gets mixed in with the turkey drippings, and I still "wash" the pan with turkey broth (or the water I plan to use in the broth) if I've already made some.
- Gravy calls for three basic ingredients: seasoned oil, flour, and rich broth.
- Make one cup of gravy by combining one tablespoon of fat, one tablespoon of flour, and one cup of broth.

Gravy Secrets

 12 servings  5 minutes 45 minutes

Preparation

- Knowing how many cups of broth you have and checking your fat content is the tricky part.
- Add some chicken broth from a can if you need more liquid.
- If you want to keep the meal on the low-fat side, you can add a bit more corn oil, or you can use the leftover broth to re-heat the turkey later.
- Good gravy can be made with a few more tips. Carefully measure the fat, then add the flour and whisk until combined before placing the pan on the stove. Ensure that the fat has completely coated the flour and that the mixture is smooth.

Gravy Secrets

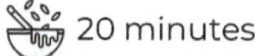 6 servings 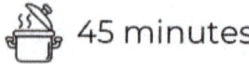 20 minutes 45 minutes

Preparation

- Next, you heat the flour-and-fat slurry until it starts to smell nutty. Mildly salty. It will have a frothy appearance and be a shade or two away from being brown.
- Then take the pan off the heat and add the liquids gradually, whisking constantly.
- Then place the pot back on the stove and heat the mixture to almost a boil.
- Just keep stirring until it reaches the desired consistency; remember, the flour has already been cooked in the fat. You can keep it on the runny side, or let it thicken up to the consistency of mashed potatoes.

Basic Turkey Gravy

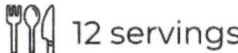 12 servings  5 minutes  45 minutes

Ingredients

- 1 Package Neck, heart, and gizzard from TURKEY giblets
- 1 Medium carrot thickly sliced
- 1 Medium onion thickly sliced
- 1 Medium celery rib thickly sliced
- 1/2 Teaspoon salt
- 1 TURKEY liver
- 3 Tablespoons fat from poultry drippings
- 3 Tablespoons all-purpose flour
- 1/2 Teaspoon salt

Preparation

- Place the neck, heart, gizzard, veggies, and salt in a 3-quart saucepan with enough water to cover and bring to a boil over high heat.
- Bring to a boil. Cover and simmer for 45 minutes on low heat.
- Cook for another 15 minutes after adding the liver. Remove the solids and pour the liquid into a large dish; refrigerate the broth.
- Once the turkey is done cooking, take it out of the pan and set it on a roasting rack. Turkey fat should be strained into a 4-cup measuring cup.
- Deglaze the roasting pan by adding 1 cup giblet broth and stirring to dislodge any crusty brown particles; then transfer the deglazed liquid to a 4-cup measuring cup. The fat will rise to the top if you let the mixture sit for a few minutes.

Basic Turkey Gravy

12 servings  5 minutes  45 minutes

Preparation

- Put a 2-quart saucepot on the stove over medium heat and add 3 tablespoons of the fat from the turkey or chicken. Into the hot fat, whisk the flour and salt, and cook while stirring until the flour turns golden.
- Meanwhile, get rid of the extra fat floating on top of the chicken fat by skimming it off. Pour the leftover broth and enough water into the turkey fat to make 3-1/2 cups.
- Slowly incorporate the hot drippings and liquid from the turkey.
- Keep stirring until the gravy comes to a boil and thickens a little.

Giblet Gravy

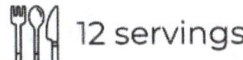 12 servings    25 minutes    45 minutes

Ingredients

- 1 Package Neck, heart, and gizzard from TURKEY giblets
- 1 Medium carrot thickly sliced
- 1 Medium onion thickly sliced
- 1 Medium celery rib thickly sliced
- 1/2 Teaspoon salt
- 1 TURKEY liver

Preparation

- Place the neck, heart, gizzard, veggies, and salt in a 3-quart saucepan with enough water to cover and bring to a boil over high heat.
- Bring to a boil. Cover and simmer for 45 minutes on low heat.
- Cook for another 15 minutes after adding the liver.
- Remove solids from the soup by straining it into a large basin, then refrigerate the broth overnight in its strained state.
- First, take the roasted turkey and roasting rack out of the roasting pan so you can create the gravy. Turkey fat should be strained into a 4-cup measuring cup.

Giblet Gravy

 12 servings   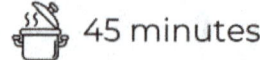 5 minutes   45 minutes

Preparation

- The fat will rise to the top if you let the mixture sit for a few minutes.
- Put a 2-quart saucepot on the stove over medium heat and add 3 tablespoons of the fat from the turkey or chicken. Into the hot fat, whisk the flour and salt, and cook while stirring until the flour turns golden.
- Meanwhile, get rid of the extra fat floating on top of the chicken fat by skimming it off.
- Pour the leftover broth and enough water into the turkey fat to make 3-1/2 cups.
- Slowly incorporate the hot drippings and liquid from the turkey.
- Discard the bones and remove the cooked meat from the neck.

Guilt-Free Turkey Gravy

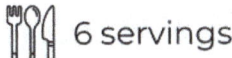 6 servings    10 minutes    15 minutes

Ingredients

- 1/4 Cup cornstarch
- 1/4 Cup water
- 4 Cups TURKEY BROTH and defatted pan juices recipe below
- Salt and pepper

Preparation

- Turkey broth and pan juices should be brought to a boil in a large saucepan over medium heat.
- While that is going on, mix the cornstarch and water until they are completely dissolved.
- Add the cornstarch mixture gradually while whisking frequently, and keep swirling until the gravy has thickened.
- To taste, season with salt and pepper.

Sweet Potato Casserole

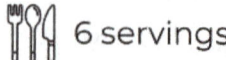 6 servings  20 minutes 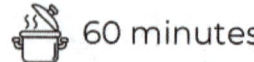 60 minutes

Ingredients

- 2 lbs. sweet potatoes, boiled, peeled and mashed
- 2 eggs, beaten 2 oz.
- margarine, melted
- 1/2 cup brown sugar
- 1 cup buttermilk
- 1/4 tsp. baking soda
- 1/2 tsp. nutmeg and cinnamon

Preparation

- Get the oven ready at 350 degrees.
- Mix everything up thoroughly. Consists of a lot of liquid.
- Prepare in an oven preheated to 350 degrees for an hour.

Mashed Sweet Potatoes

 6 servings  15 minutes  45 minutes

Ingredients

- 4 medium sweet potatoes, peeled
- 1 tbsp. butter
- 1/4 cup milk
- 3/8 cup brown sugar
- 1 tsp. cinnamon

Preparation

- Put water on to boil.
- Cube up some peeled and cubed potatoes.
- Just add to the pot of boiling water. Wait until the potatoes are tender before serving.
- Take potatoes out and put them in a bowl.
- Perform the mash with a mixer or potato masher.
- Stir in the butter and milk.
- Combine the brown sugar and cinnamon and mix to combine.
- To serve, pour into a dish.
- Cinnamon powder can be used.

Roast Garlic Mashed Potatoes

 6 servings   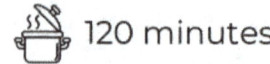 20 minutes   120 minutes

Ingredients

- 8 to 10 cloves garlic, peeled
- 1 cup olive oil
- 4 russet potatoes
- 2 tbsp. butter
- 1/3 to 1/2 cup heavy cream
- 1/4 cup Asiago cheese, grated 2 tbsp.
- Parmigiano-Reggiano cheese, grated
- Salt and pepper, to taste

Preparation

- Heat the olive oil and garlic in a large saucepan over the lowest possible heat for 30–40 minutes, or until the garlic is tender.
- Take out the trash (reserve for marinades or vinaigrettes).
- Separate the garlic and purée it.
- In the meantime, bake the potatoes at 400 degrees Fahrenheit for an hour, or until tender. Peel and mash while still hot, or run through a potato ricer.
- Garlic purée and butter should be melted together with heavy cream.
- Cook with seasoning and potatoes.
- Include cheeses and season with salt and pepper.
- Transfer to a gratin dish with a spoon.
- Bake for 12-15 minutes at 400°F, until golden and bubbling.

Crockpot Scalloped Potatoes

 9 servings  10 minutes 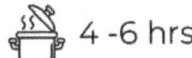 4 -6 hrs

Ingredients

- 6-8 thinly sliced potatoes
- 1 can cheddar cheese soup
- 1 cup velveeta cheese
- 1-1/2 cups grated sharp cheddar cheese
- 1 can (12 oz.) evaporated milk
- Salt and pepper

Preparation

- Coat the inside of the slow cooker with cooking spray.
- Half-fill the slow cooker with the cut potatoes.
- Place a half can of soup, a half cup of Velveeta cheese (chunky), a 3/4 cup of shredded sharp cheese, and a half can of milk in a casserole dish and layer.
- Season to taste with salt and pepper.
- Remaining components should be layered in the same fashion.
- Heat for roughly 6 hours on high. You may want to taste it to see if extra milk is needed. To save time, boil the potatoes ahead of time.

Squash Casserole

 6 servings   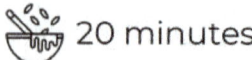 20 minutes    30 minutes

Ingredients

- 4 cups cooked yellow crook neck squash
- 1 medium onion
- 1 tsp salt
- 1/2 tsp pepper
- 1 stick butter or margarine
- 2 cups crushed Cheezit crackers
- 2 cups shredded cheddar cheese
- 1 cup milk or heavy cream

Preparation

- When the onion and squash are soft, season with salt and pepper and cook in a pan with butter.
- Combine everything else, save for the reserved crackers and cheese, in a large mixing bowl.
- Toss with the remaining crackers and cheese and pour into a 2-quart casserole.
- Set oven temperature to 350 degrees and bake for 30 minutes.

Stuffed Acorn Squash

🍴 6 servings   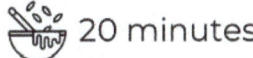 20 minutes    30 minutes

Ingredients

- 2 acorn squash
- 2 carrots, grated 1 can (8 oz.)
- crushed pineapple 2 tbsp.
- dried white raisins
- 1/4 tsp. ginger

Preparation

- Squash should be halved and the seeds removed. Arrange in a pan for the oven.
- Mix the remaining ingredients and stuff the squash with them.
- For 30 minutes at 350 degrees, or until squash is soft.

Ice Cream Pumpkin Pie

 6 servings 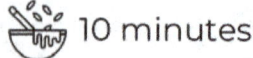 10 minutes 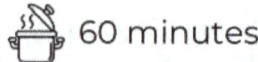 60 minutes

Ingredients

- 1 package (9 ounces) prepared graham cracker pie crust
- 1-pint vanilla ice cream softened
- 1 can (16 ounces) pumpkin
- 1 cup whipped cream
- 3/4 cup sugar
- 2 teaspoons pumpkin pie spice
- 1/2 teaspoon salt

Preparation

- Freeze ice cream in pie crust until it can be cut with a knife.
- Mix pumpkin, whipped cream, sugar, pumpkin pie spice, and salt in a medium bowl.
- Add the mixture to the ice cream in the crust and freeze until solid.
- When ready to serve, take pie out of freezer and let thaw in fridge for at least an hour. Cut into wedges and serve with extra whipped topping.

Pumpkin Cake Roll

 16 servings    5 minutes   15 minutes

Ingredients

Cake:
- 3 eggs -- room temp.
- 1 cup sugar
- 2/3 cup canned pumpkin
- 1 teaspoon lemon juice
- 3/4 cup flour
- 1 teaspoon baking powder
- 2 teaspoons cinnamon
- 1 teaspoon ginger
- 1/2 teaspoon nutmeg
- 1/2 teaspoon salt
- 1 cup walnuts, chopped

Filling:
- 1 cup confectioners' sugar
- 6 ounces of cream cheese
- 4 teaspoons butter
- 1/2 teaspoon vanilla

Pumpkin Cake Roll

 16 servings  5 minutes 15 minutes

Preparation

- Whisk eggs for 5 minutes.
- Beat in sugar, pumpkin, and lemon juice gradually. Flour, baking powder, spices, and salt should be combined in a separate bowl. Blend into the pumpkin sauce. Distribute in a jelly-roll pan that has been previously prepared.
- Put chopped walnuts on top
- Put in the oven and bake for 15 minutes at 375 degrees Fahrenheit.
- Dump the cake onto a towel, dust it with confectioners' sugar, and roll jelly-roll style.
- Cool.
- Cream together the filling's components.
- In order to re-roll the cake with the filling, unroll it.

Pumpkin and Praline Pie

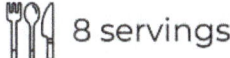 8 servings  30 minutes  55 minutes

Ingredients

- 2 pie crusts
- Filling:
- 1/2 cup sugar
- 1/2 cup light brown sugar
- 1 tbsp. flour
- 1 tbsp. bitters (optional)
- 1 tsp. cinnamon
- 1 tsp. ginger
- 1/2 tsp. salt
- 1/4 tsp. nutmeg
- 1/4 tsp. cloves
- 1 egg, lightly beaten
- 2 tbsp. butter

Preparation

- Praline:
- Get the crusts ready.
- Prepare a temperature of 450 degrees Fahrenheit.
- Each crust should have a quarter of the praline filling. It takes around 10 minutes in the oven to get the praline bubbling and golden.
- Make sure the oven is only at 400 degrees.
- Spoon one-half of the pumpkin filling into each pie crust and level the surface.
- Pumpkin should be firm and crusts should be golden after about an hour in the oven. When ready to serve, allow it cool to room temperature.
- If desired, serve with whipped cream or another topping.

Famous Pumpkin Nut Bread

🍴 8 servings  20 minutes 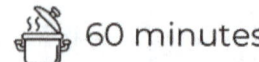 60 minutes

Ingredients

- 1 cup butter, melted
- 4 eggs
- 1 can (14-1/2 oz.) pumpkin
- 1/2 tsp. salt
- 2 tsp. baking powder
- 1 tsp. baking soda
- 1 tsp. ground cloves
- 1 tsp. ground nutmeg
- 1 tsp. ground cinnamon
- 1 cup sugar
- 1 cup brown sugar
- 2-3/4 cups flour
- 1 cup chopped nuts

Preparation

- Mix in eggs and pumpkin. Thoroughly beat them.
- Sprinkle in the sugars, baking soda, baking powder, and spices. Remove any lumps by beating them vigorously.
- Include flour. Completely beat them up.
- Toss in some nuts and combine.
- Pour into 2 greased loaf pans.
- Cook at 350 degrees for 1 hour. Check the doneness of the loaves using a toothpick.

Barbecued Turkey With Maple-Mustard Sauce

 8 servings  20 minutes 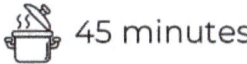 45 minutes

Ingredients

For turkey:
- 6 quarts water
- 2 large onions(quartered)
- 1 cup coarse salt
- 1 cup chopped fresh ginger
- 3/4 cup (packed) golden brown sugar
- 4 large bay leaves
- 4 whole star anise
- 12 whole black peppercorns(crushed).
- 1 13- to 14-pound turkey, niblets discarded.
- 4 cups hickory smoke chips(soaked in water 30 minutes, drained)
- Disposable 9x6 1/4x1-inch aluminium broiler pans.
- 2 large oranges, cut into wedges
- 1/4 cup olive oil
- 2 tablespoons oriental sesame oil.

For glaze:
- 3/4 cup pure maple syrup, 1/2 cup dry white wine
- 1/3 cup Dijon mustard
- 2 tablespoons (1/4 stick) butter.

Barbecued Turkey With Maple-Mustard Sauce

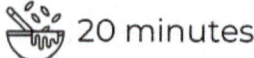 8 servings  20 minutes 45 minutes

Preparation

- Before anything else, the turkey spends an entire night in a brine that enhances its flavour and keeps the meat tender. (Use a saucepan big enough to fit the turkey and the brine.)
- Napa Valley staples wine and mustard are used in the sweet, tangy glaze that perfectly complements the smokiness of the turkey.
- Refrigerate the brine until it is totally cold. Wash the turkey thoroughly, inside and out.
- Put the turkey in the brine and press down to immerse it. Toss the turkey in the marinade and chill it twice before serving.
- If grilling with charcoal:
- Fill the barbecue with a mound of charcoal and let it burn until it's a pale grey. Toss the heated briquettes into two heaps, one on each side of the grill, using tongs. Incorporate a hearty 1/2 cup of hickory chips into each mound.
- Between the stacks, put the broiler pan. Make sure the grill is raised above the briquettes by at least 6 inches.
- The barbeque vents should be set up such that the chips smoke and the briquettes burn without igniting.

Barbecued Turkey With Maple-Mustard Sauce

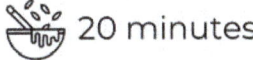 8 servings   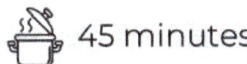 20 minutes   45 minutes

Preparation

- For a grilling session with gas or electricity:
- Turn all burners high in order to preheat the grill. Switch to medium-low heat on the perimeter burners and turn off the central burner.
- Ample 1/2 cups of hickory chips should be spread out between 2 broiler pans. The cookware should be placed over two active burners.
- Prepare an empty broiling pan for use over a turned-off stovetop burner. Keep the grill above the burners by at least six inches.
- Taking the turkey out of the brine and throwing it away. Wash and dry the turkey with paper towels. Fill the main cavity with orange wedges.
- Combo the olive oil and the sesame oil in a little basin. The turkey can be ignored.
- Put on the grill, breast side up, in the middle, directly over the empty broiler pan. For roughly three hours, covered, add 1 cup of hickory chips (and 6 briquettes if using charcoal) to the barbeque every 30 minutes until an instant-read thermometer placed into the thickest portion of the thigh registers 160°F.

Barbecued Turkey With Maple-Mustard Sauce

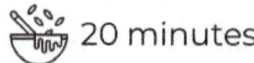 8 servings    20 minutes   45 minutes

Preparation

- To make a glaze:
- Simmer the mixture in a heavy medium-sized pot.
- Glaze the turkey, then cover and continue cooking until an instant-read thermometer put into the centre of the thickest portion of the thigh reads 180 degrees Fahrenheit (approximately 1 hour longer).
- Gather the turkey on a serving plate. Wrap in foil and leave to rest for 30 minutes. Eats 8!

Thanksgiving Turkey

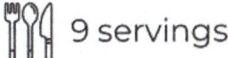 9 servings    50 minutes    4-6 hrs

Ingredients

- 1 turkey
- 1/2cup butter
- 2(12 fluid ounce) canscola-flavored carbonated beverage
- 1 apple(quartered)
- 1 onion(chopped)
- 1tablespoon garlic powder
- 1tablespoon salt, 1tablespoon ground black pepper
- 4cloves crushed garlic
- 1tablespoon salt.

Preparation

- Fire up a charcoal or gas grill to 375 degrees F (110 to 120 degrees C)
- Take out the turkey's guts and save them for gravy if you like.
- Use cold water to wash the turkey, then pat it dry.
- Stuff the turkey with butter (or margarine), cola, apple, onion, garlic powder, salt, and black pepper. Use smashed garlic to rub all over the bird's exterior before seasoning with salt.
- Cover the turkey loosely with foil and place it in a 10x15-inch roasting pan.
- Until an interior temperature of 180 degrees F has been reached, smoke at 225 to 250 degrees F (110 to 120 degrees C) for 10 hours (80 degrees C).

Five Spiced Turkey

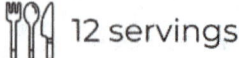 12 servings 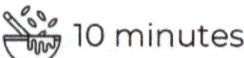 10 minutes  25 minutes

Ingredients

- 6 tablespoons low-sodium soya sauce
- 1 tablespoon garlic powder
- 1 teaspoon ground ginger
- 2 teaspoons paprika
- 1 tablespoon fresh chopped basil
- 2 teaspoon parsley
- 1/4 tsp black pepper
- 2 teaspoons Chinese five-spice powder
- 1 (12-pound) turkey, water.

Preparation

- In a small bowl, whisk together the soy sauce, garlic powder, ginger powder, paprika powder, basil powder, parsley powder, pepper powder, and five-spice powder.
- Take the turkey apart and get rid of the neck and the giblets.
- Salt and pepper the inside and outside of the turkey after it has been thoroughly cleaned and dried.
- Pour half of the marinade over the turkey and set the other half aside.
- Set roasting rack in place and place turkey on it. To preheat the roaster, add roughly a cup of water to the bottom.
- Make a tent out of foil to cover the roasting.

Five Spiced Turkey

 12 servings    10 minutes    25 minutes

Preparation

- In a small bowl, whisk together the soy sauce, garlic powder, ginger powder, paprika powder, basil powder, parsley powder, pepper powder, and five-spice powder.
- Take the turkey apart and get rid of the neck and the giblets.
- Salt and pepper the inside and outside of the turkey after it has been thoroughly cleaned and dried.
- Pour half of the marinade over the turkey and set the other half aside.
- Set roasting rack in place and place turkey on it. To preheat the roaster, add roughly a cup of water to the bottom.
- Make a tent out of foil to cover the roasting.

Five Spiced Turkey

🍴 12 servings  10 minutes  25 minutes

Preparation

- Cover the turkey with the tent and make sure the sides are sealed by spraying the underside with nonstick cooking spray.
- To achieve a golden brown crust, roast a turkey at 325 degrees for about 15 minutes per pound, basting often.
- Take turkey out of oven, let it rest for 10 minutes, then place on tray and serve with marinade on the side.
- Produces around 12–14 portions.

Bread And Oyster Stuffing

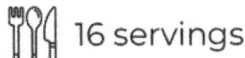 16 servings  15 minutes  50 minutes

Ingredients

- 1 pound white bread slices(dried in a 250° oven for 1 hour, about 10 to 12 cups torn)
- 3/4 cup butter or margarine
- 2 cups finely chopped celery
- 2 cups finely chopped onion
- 1/2 cup milk, scalded
- 3 containers of fresh or canned oysters (16 to 24 ounces total) drained
- 1 teaspoon lemon juice
- 1/4 teaspoon salt
- 3/4 teaspoon poultry seasoning
- 1/4 teaspoon black pepper.

Preparation

- Fry the onion and celery in the butter until they are tender.
- Crumble the dry bread into a large bowl and stir with the warm milk.
- The oysters should be added to the mixture of onion and celery that has been drained.
- Make sure to stir the components together very carefully. Season with salt, pepper, poultry seasoning, and lemon juice.
- Blend carefully yet thoroughly.

Green Onion And Cornbread Stuffing

12 servings   5 minutes   45 minutes

Ingredients

- 1 Can (10-1/2 ounces) condensed French onion soup
- Soup Can water, 1/4 Cup margarine
- 1 Cup celery cut into 1/4-inch cubes
- 1 Cup green onions thinly sliced
- 1-1/2 Teaspoons poultry seasoning
- 2 Packages (8 ounces each) of cornbread stuffing mix, Vegetable cooking spray.

Preparation

- Get the oven ready at 350 degrees. Put the soup, water, margarine, celery, onions, and poultry spice into a 5-quart pot and stir to mix.
- Bring to a boil, then turn off heat.
- Stuffing mix made from cornmeal should be added and mixed in.
- Put stuffing in a 1-1/2 quart casserole dish sprayed with vegetable cooking spray and bake.
- Cover and bake in a preheated 350°F oven for 45 minutes, or until firm.

Pecan Pumpkin Pie

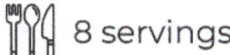 8 servings    15 minutes    50 minutes

Ingredients

- 3 eggs
- 1 cup solid pack of pumpkin
- 1/3 cup sugar
- 1 teaspoon pumpkin pie spice
- 2/3 cup corn syrup
- ½ cup sugar
- 3 tablespoons melted butter
- ½ teaspoon vanilla
- 1 cup pecan halves
- 1 unbaked 9-inch pastry shell.

Preparation

- Pumpkin, 1/3 cup sugar, and pie spice should be combined with one barely beaten egg.
- Use to coat the bottom of the pie plate.
- Mix together 2 beaten eggs, the corn syrup, 1/2 cup sugar, the butter, and the vanilla extract. Incorporate the nuts into the mixture.
- Pour over the pumpkin filling.
- Filling should be set after 50 minutes in a moderate oven (350 degrees).

Thanksgiving Cranberry Relish

🍴 8 servings    10 minutes    120 minutes

Ingredients

- 4 c. cranberries
- 2 oranges
- 1 1/2 c. sugar.

Preparation

- Scrub the oranges and cranberries.
- Core and quarter your oranges.
- Put the cranberries and oranges through the blender or food processor.
- Blend in some sugar, please.
- To get the greatest results, start working on this at least two days before Thanksgiving.

Easy Pumpkin Cake

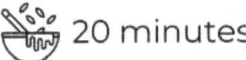 6 servings    20 minutes   55 minutes

Ingredients

- 1 1/4 cups sliced almonds
- 3 eggs
- 1 16-ounce can of pumpkin (not pumpkin pie filling)
- 1 tablespoon pumpkin pie spice
- 1/2 cup vegetable oil
- 1 package yellow cake mix (1 pound, 2 1/4 ounces)
- 1 teaspoon grated orange peel
- Orange glaze (see below).

Preparation

- Prepare a 350-degree oven.
- The almonds should be spread out in a single layer in a shallow pan.
- To toast, put in a cold oven and bake for 9-11 minutes at 350 degrees, stirring occasionally.
- Cool. Butter spray your Bundt pan with cooking spray, and then coat it with 1/2 cup of almonds. Eggs, pumpkin, spices, and oil should all be mixed together in an electric mixer.
- Incorporate cake mix.
- To make a smoother mixture, beat for 2 minutes on medium speed.
- Mix in the remaining 3/4 cup of almonds and the orange peel.

Easy Pumpkin Cake

 6 servings  20 minutes 55 minutes

Preparation

- Put the liquid into the pan.
- Put into an oven that has been warmed to 375 degrees and bake for 45 to 55 minutes, or until a pick inserted in the centre comes out clean.
- Cool. Flip onto a serving platter and sprinkle with orange glaze. Produces 10-12 portions.

Thanksgiving Muffins

 6 servings    15 minutes    25 minutes

Ingredients

- 1 cup cooked pumpkin or canned
- 1/2 cup sugar
- 1/2 cup margarine
- 1 egg, beaten
- 1 tablespoon molasses
- 2 cups sifted flour(sift before measuring)
- 1/4 teaspoon cloves
- 1/4 teaspoon nutmeg
- 1/4 teaspoon cinnamon
- 1/4 teaspoon mace
- 1 teaspoon baking powder
- 1 teaspoon salt
- 1 teaspoon soda
- 3/4 cup buttermilk
- 1/2 cup chopped pecans
- 1/2 cup raisins.

Thanksgiving Muffins

 6 servings    15 minutes   25 minutes

Preparation

- Cream together the sugar and margarine.
- Mix in the egg, molasses, and pumpkin.
- Combine baking soda, baking powder, and seasonings into flour, and sift.
- Mix baking soda into buttermilk.
- Using 1/2 cup of sifted flour and spices, combine raisins and nuts.
- To the creamed mixture, add the remaining flour, alternating with the buttermilk.
- Toss in some raisins and chopped nuts.
- Put into muffin tins that have been generously buttered. Cook for 20 minutes at 375 degrees. In a really large pan, baking time could be as little as 25 minutes.
- It's enough for 2 dozen regular-sized muffins or 4 dozen mini muffins.

Thanksgiving Ambrosia

 8 servings  10 minutes 60 minutes

Ingredients

- 2 grapefruit(sectioned)
- 3 oranges(sectioned)
- 2 tangerines(sectioned)
- 1/3 to 1/2 c. sugar
- 1/2 c. shredded coconut.

Preparation

- Divide the fruit in halves and arrange it on a serving dish, then sprinkle with sugar and coconut.
- Combining the remaining fruit, sugar, and coconut is the final step.
- Be sure to chill for at least an hour before serving. Prepares 8 servings.

Thanksgiving Pumpkin Bread

🍴 6 servings  15 minutes  75 minutes

Ingredients

- 1 1/2 c. pumpkin
- 3/4 c. vegetable oil, 2 1/2 c. flour
- 2 c. sugar
- 1 1/2 tsp. baking soda
- 1 1/4 tsp. salt
- 3/4 tsp. nutmeg 3
- /4 tsp. cinnamon
- 1 c. nuts chopped
- 1 c. raisin
- 3 1 lb. coffee cans.

Preparation

- The oven needs to be heated to 350 degrees.
- The result is three loaves.
- Mix these: 1 The pumpkin is a half cup in size. Oil from vegetable sources, around 3/4 cup
- Next, insert: 2 1/4 cups of sugar Measure out 2 cups of sugar. Half a teaspoon of baking soda 1 and a quarter gramme of salt Nutmeg, about 3/4 of a teaspoon About half a teaspoon of cinnamon 1/2 tsp. ground nutmeg 1 cup of raisins, optional
- Combine the ingredients and stir until they are well moistened.
- Half-fill three un-greased one-pound coffee cans.

Thanksgiving Pumpkin Bread

 6 servings    15 minutes    75 minutes

Preparation

- Put into the oven and bake for 75 minutes at 350 degrees.
- Remove from the can after cooling for 15 minutes.
- Seal in aluminium foil while it's still hot. Refrigerating is optional but recommended.
- Toast it in the toaster or microwave it in slices.

Cranberry Sauce

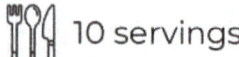 10 servings  5 minutes  15 minutes

Ingredients

- 1-1/2 C sugar
- 1 navel orange
- 1/2 t grated ginger
- 4 cup cranberries
- 1/2 C (2 oz.) toasted pecans.

Preparation

- Orange peel, grated, is added to sugar and ginger in a simmering pot.
- Simmer the orange juice and sugar over low heat until the sugar is dissolved.
- For about 5 minutes, after adding the cranberries, you should hear them pop.
- Sprinkle in the pecans, and set the sauce in the fridge to cool.

Garlic Mashed Potatoes

 4 servings    10 minutes    45 minutes

Ingredients

- 8 potatoes(peeled and quartered)
- 1/2 cup milk
- 1/4 cup butter
- 2 cloves garlic minced
- salt to taste
- 1 pinch of ground white pepper
- 2 tablespoons sesame seeds.

Preparation

- To cook potatoes, bring a big pot of water to a boil, then add them and cook for 20–25 minutes, or until tender.
- Then, transfer the drained pasta to a big basin.
- Milk, butter, garlic, salt, and pepper can be added to the potatoes as well.
- The consistency can be adjusted by using a hand mixer, electric mixer, or potato masher.
- Add some sesame seeds for flavour.

Holiday Turkey with Michigan Maple Glaze and Cranberry Bourbon Relish

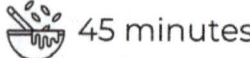 12 servings  45 minutes 180 minutes

Ingredients

- 1 whole 12-15 lb. fresh turkey
- salt and pepper to taste
- 1 onion
- 3-4 T. unsalted butter, melted
- 2 C. chicken stock
- 1/4 C. maple syrup
- cranberry-bourbon relish (recipe follows)

Preparation

- Prepare a 350°F oven. Wash the turkey thoroughly, inside and out.
- Prepare the inside and outside by seasoning with salt and pepper.
- Insert the onion, close the opening with a skewer, and secure the legs with string.
- In a big roasting pan with a rack, position the turkey so that the breast is facing up.
- Coat the turkey with half of the melted butter.
- Add half a cup of stock to the pan.
-

Holiday Turkey with Michigan Maple Glaze and Cranberry Bourbon Relish

 12 servings  45 minutes 180 minutes

Preparation

- A meat thermometer should read 180 degrees Fahrenheit in the thigh and 170 degrees Fahrenheit in the breast for an ideal turkey (about 3 hours).
- Add 1/2 cup of stock to the pan and baste the turkey with the juices every 45 minutes.
- Brush the turkey with a mixture of the remaining butter and maple syrup during the last half an hour of cooking.

Cranberry Bourbon Relish

 6 servings    15 minutes   15 minutes

Ingredients

- 2 C. bourbon
- 1/2 C. minced shallot
- zest 1 large orange
- 2 (12 oz.) bags of fresh cranberries
- 2 C. sugar
- 1 t. freshly grated ginger
- 2 t. ground black pepper

Preparation

- In a saucepan (not metal), mix the bourbon, shallots, ginger, and orange zest.
- Cook at high heat until it reaches a rolling boil, then reduce heat and simmer until it reaches a syrupy glaze consistency (about 10 minutes).
- Increase the heat, and bring the cranberries and sugar to a boil while stirring constantly.
- Reduce heat and simmer until cranberries begin to burst about 5 minutes.
- Turn off the stove and season with pepper.
- Put in the fridge until ready to use.
- It's plenty for eight to ten people.

Apricot Honey Ham Glaze

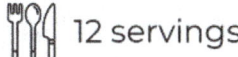 12 servings  5 minutes  5 minutes

Ingredients

- 1/2 cup apricot preserves
- 1/2 cup honey
- 1 tablespoon cornstarch
- 3 tablespoons lemon juice
- 1/4 teaspoon ground cloves

Preparation

- How to Make Ham Glaze:
- In a saucepan over medium heat, mix all ham glaze ingredients.
- Bring to a boil and keep stirring until it thickens and begins to bubble.
- Baste the ham with the glaze every 10 minutes for the final 30 minutes of baking.
- Prepares 1 cup of ham glaze.

Glazed Baked Ham

 40 servings    30 minutes   240 minutes

Ingredients

- 1/3 cup light brown sugar, packed
- 1/2 cup honey
- 1/3 cup dry red wine
- 1/2 cup pineapple juice
- 1 medium clove garlic, finely minced
- 1 fully cooked ham, about 6 pounds

Preparation

- Brown sugar, honey, wine, pineapple juice, and minced garlic should be mixed in a large basin or food storage bag large enough to hold a ham.
- Marinate ham in the fridge for 6+ hours (overnight is best) by placing it in the marinade and turning it to coat it well.
- The oven needs to be preheated to 350 degrees.
- Roast the ham with the marinade you saved basting it every 20 minutes.
- When a meat thermometer inserted away from the bone registers 140 degrees, the ham is done baking; this should take around 10 minutes per pound.
- Approximately 8-10 people can be fed.

Best Pickled Eggs

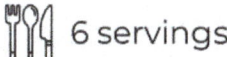 6 servings    5 minutes    15 minutes

Ingredients

- 12 eggs
- 4 cups distilled white vinegar
- 6 cloves garlic
- 1 tablespoon whole white peppercorns
- 1 tablespoon whole allspice
- 2 slices fresh ginger root (optional)

Preparation

- Place eggs in a saucepan and cover with water.
- Bring to a boil.
- Cover, remove from heat, and let eggs sit in hot water for 10 to 12 minutes.
- Cool in cold water and peel.
- In a saucepan, combine vinegar, garlic, peppercorns and allspice.
- Add sliced ginger if desired.
- Simmer for 10 minutes.
- Place eggs in sterilized preserving jars.
- Pour vinegar mixture over eggs; strain if desired.
- Seal and immerse jars in a preserving saucepan with a rack to hold jars with at least 1-inch water above the tops of jars. Cover and boil for 10 minutes.
- Remove jars and cool.

Best Pickled Eggs

 6 servings    5 minutes   15 minutes

Preparation

- Check seals, the lid should not move at all when pressed.
- Store about one month before opening.

Buttermilk Corn Fritters

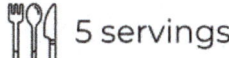 5 servings 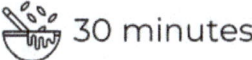 30 minutes  30 minutes

Ingredients

- 1 1/3 cups buttermilk baking mix
- 1 1/2 teaspoons baking powder
- 1 (14.75 ounces) can of cream-style corn
- 1 egg, beaten
- 1 cup vegetable oil
- 1 1/2 cups maple syrup

Preparation

- Sift the baking mix and baking powder together in a large mixing dish.
- Corn and egg should be mixed in a small basin.
- Add the eggs to the flour and stir carefully.
- Oil a big skillet and place it over medium heat.
- Put the batter in the oil in a single layer using a tablespoon.
- To achieve a golden brown colour, fry for 2 minutes per side.
- Absorbent paper fritters in the drain.
- Quickly drizzle on some maple syrup or molasses and serve.

Cheese Ball

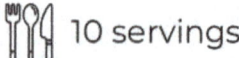 10 servings  15 minutes  15 minutes

Ingredients

- 2 (8-ounce) packages of cream cheese
- 1 (8-ounce) can crush pineapple, drained
- 1 tablespoon diced onion
- 1 tablespoon chopped green bell pepper
- 1/4 tablespoon seasoning salt
- 1 cup chopped pecans

Preparation

- In a large mixing bowl, combine the cream cheese, pineapple, onion, bell pepper, and seasoning salt.
- Roll the ball in the chopped pecans and shape it into a cookie. Toss with butter crackers and refrigerate.

Cheese Fondue

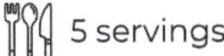 5 servings  5 minutes  10 minutes

Ingredients

- 1 cup dry white wine
- 1/2 pound shredded Swiss cheese
- 1/2 pound shredded Gruyere cheese
- 2 tablespoons all-purpose flour
- 1/4 teaspoon salt
- 1/4 teaspoon ground nutmeg
- 1 (1 pound) loaf of French bread, cut into 1-inch cubes

Preparation

- Warm the wine in the fondue pot over low heat.
- Sprinkle in Swiss cheese and Gruyere cheese, a quarter pound at a time.
- Until the cheese has melted, stirring after each addition.
- Blend in some flour and mix it all.
- Add the salt and nutmeg and mix in once the cheese has melted.
- To accompany, use cubes of French bread.

Cheeseball II

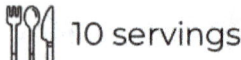 10 servings  15 minutes  15 minutes

Ingredients

- 1 (8-ounce) package of cream cheese
- 8 ounces shredded Cheddar cheese
- 1 (8-ounce) package of shredded Monterey Jack cheese
- 1 teaspoon monosodium glutamate (MSG)
- 1 teaspoon Worcestershire sauce
- 1 (6 ounces) package of sliced ham, chopped
- 6 ounces of thin-sliced beef luncheon meat

Preparation

- Mix cream cheese, Cheddar cheese, Jack cheese, monosodium glutamate, Worcestershire sauce, ham, and beef together.
- Get everything well-mixed, and roll it into a ball.
- Put it in the fridge and let it cold.

Corn Fritters

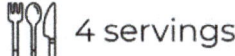 4 servings  10 minutes  20 minutes

Ingredients

- 3 cups oil for frying
- 1 cup sifted all-purpose flour
- 1 teaspoon baking powder
- 1/2 teaspoon salt
- 1/4 teaspoon white sugar
- 1 egg, lightly beaten
- 1/2 cup milk
- 1 tablespoon shortening, melted
- 1 (12 ounces) can whole kernel corn, drained

Preparation

- To prepare, bring oil to 365 degrees Fahrenheit in a large saucepan or deep fryer (185 degrees C).
- Put the flour, baking soda, salt, and sugar in a medium bowl and mix them.
- In a separate bowl, combine the egg, milk, and melted shortening and then beat into the flour mixture.
- Add the corn to the mixture.
- Place heaping tablespoons of fritter batter into the hot oil and cook, turning once, until golden.
- Pour the waste into some paper towels.

Creamy Cheddar Cheese Soup

🍴 6 servings   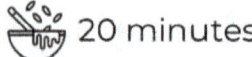 20 minutes    30 minutes

Ingredients

- 1/4 cup butter
- 1 onion, chopped
- 1/4 cup all-purpose flour
- 3 cups chicken broth
- 3 cups milk
- 1 pound shredded Cheddar cheese

Preparation

- Butter or margarine should be melted in a 3-quart saucepan set over medium heat.
- After about 5 minutes, add the onion, and cook until it's soft.
- Add the flour and continue cooking until it has absorbed the onion flavour.
- Once the mixture has thickened a bit, add the chicken broth and continue cooking it while stirring regularly.
- Stirring frequently, bringing the milk to a boil.
- About a quarter of the soup mixture at a time should be blended until smooth in a covered blender on medium speed.

Creamy Cheddar Cheese Soup

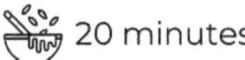 6 servings  20 minutes 30 minutes

Preparation

- Put back into the pan and bring to a boil over medium heat.
- Take it off the heat.
- To melt the cheese, mix it in with a wire whisk or a slotted spoon.
- If the cheese is not entirely melted after being heated for 1 minute over low heat while being stirred regularly, repeat the process.

Deviled Eggs

🍴 6 servings  12 minutes  35 minutes

Ingredients

- 8 eggs
- 1/2 teaspoon prepared mustard
- 1 tablespoon creamy salad dressing
- salt and pepper to taste
- 1 pinch paprika

Preparation

- Add water to a pot large enough to hold the eggs, and set over medium heat.
- The water should be brought to a boil.
- Keep the eggs in hot water for 10 to 12 minutes, covered and off the stove.
- Take the item out of the boiling water and let it cool.
- Remove the skin and slice the fruit in half lengthwise.
- Take out the eggs' yellows and mix them in a bowl with some mustard, salad dressing, and seasonings.
- Combine and blend thoroughly.
- Sprinkle paprika on top of the egg halves, then fill with the yolk mixture.

Pickled Pumpkin

 9 servings 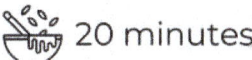 20 minutes 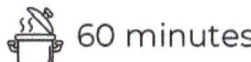 60 minutes

Ingredients

- 4 pounds peeled and diced pumpkin
- 5 cups white sugar
- 5 cups distilled white vinegar
- 4 cinnamon sticks
- 15 whole cloves

Preparation

- Place the pumpkin in a very large and deep bowl.
- Combine sugar, vinegar, cinnamon sticks, and cloves in a big saucepan.
- Put on high heat for 5 minutes.
- Toss the pumpkin in the bowl with the hot liquid.
- Set aside for 8 hours, or overnight, covered.
- Pour the liquid through a strainer into a big pot.
- Prepare by bringing it to a boil for five minutes.
- Take out the cloves and cinnamon sticks, but keep a few sprigs for garnish.
- Return the pumpkin to the liquid and bring it to a boil once more.
- The pumpkin should be cooked for 5 minutes at a high boil until it is translucent and yet slightly crunchy.
- Please wait while I let the mixture cool.

Frosted Pecan Bites

 10 servings 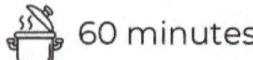 5 minutes 60 minutes

Ingredients

- 8 ounces of feta cheese, crumbled
- 3 tablespoons finely chopped green onions
- 1 egg, beaten
- 1 (17.5 ounces) package of frozen puff pastry, thawed
- 1 egg yolk, beaten with 1 teaspoon water

Preparation

- The oven should be heated to 375 degrees F. (190 degrees C).
- Combine feta cheese, green onions, and egg in a separate bowl.
- Square off a sheet of pastry to make 12 servings.
- In the middle of each square, mound 1 tablespoon of the feta mixture.
- Wet the outer edges of the pastry and fold it over the filling to make a triangle.
- Seal the edges by pressing them together firmly with a fork.
- Use the egg yolk mixture to lightly brush the pastries.
- Put into an oven that has been prepared to 400 degrees and bake for 20 minutes.
- Whether served warm or at room temperature, this dish is sure to please.

Fruit Dip

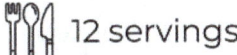 12 servings  5 minutes  120 minutes

Ingredients

- 8 ounces of cream cheese
- 1/2 cup marshmallow creme
- 2 cups frozen whipped topping, thawed
- 1/4 cup unsweetened pineapple juice

Preparation

- Combine softened topping, marshmallow creme, and cream cheese in a blender.
- The consistency should be that of a dip, so add some pineapple juice.
- Let it rest in the fridge for an hour.

Mini Sweet Potato Pies

🍴 6 servings   🥣 15 minutes   🍲 30 minutes

Ingredients

- 3/4 pound sweet potato, peeled and diced
- 1 (9-inch) refrigerated pie crust
- 3/4 cup evaporated skim milk
- 2 egg whites
- 1/4 cup white sugar
- 2 tablespoons brown sugar
- 3/4 teaspoon ground cinnamon
- 1/8 teaspoon ground nutmeg
- 1/8 teaspoon ground cloves
- 1/4 cup halved cranberries (optional)

Mini Sweet Potato Pies

 6 servings  15 minutes 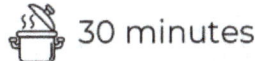 30 minutes

Preparation

- Put the sweet potato in a saucepan and add enough water to cover it.
- The recommended cooking time is 5 minutes at a rolling boil, or until the food can be easily pierced with a fork.
- Mash with a fork or potato masher after draining.
- To bake, heat the oven to 425 degrees F. (220 degrees C).
- Form 24 individual dough balls using the pie crust.
- Tartlet shells can be made by pressing the dough into two 12-cup mini muffin tins. Leave aside.

Mini Sweet Potato Pies

 6 servings 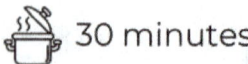 15 minutes 30 minutes

Preparation

- Add the sweet potato, evaporated milk, egg whites, white sugar, brown sugar, cinnamon, nutmeg, and cloves to a blender or food processor and pulse until smooth.
- Blend till silky smooth. Fill each tart shell with about 1 spoonful of the ingredients.
- If a toothpick inserted into the centre of one of the tarts comes out clean after 10 minutes in the preheated oven, the tarts are done. Let the pans sit on a wire rack to cool. Put half a cranberry on top of each tart before serving.

Pumpkin Dip

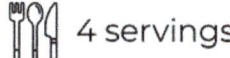 4 servings  15 minutes  15 minutes

Ingredients

- 1 (8-ounce) package of cream cheese, softened
- 2 cups confectioners' sugar
- 1 (15-ounce) can solid pack of pumpkin
- 1 tablespoon ground cinnamon
- 1 tablespoon pumpkin pie spice
- 1 teaspoon frozen orange juice concentrate

Preparation

- Cream cheese and powdered sugar should be mixed until smooth in a medium bowl.
- Slowly incorporate the pumpkin.
- Orange juice, cinnamon, and pumpkin pie spice should be stirred in until smooth and incorporated.
- Place in the fridge until ready to serve.

Roasted Pumpkin Seeds

 6 servings    5 minutes   45 minutes

Ingredients

- 1 1/2 cups raw whole pumpkin seeds
- 2 teaspoons butter, melted
- 1 pinch salt

Preparation

- The oven should be heated to 300 degrees F. (150 degrees C).
- Combine the seeds with the melted butter and the salt in a bowl and toss.
- For best results, spread the seeds out in a single layer on a baking sheet and bake at 300° for 45 minutes, stirring occasionally.

Sausage Balls

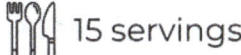 15 servings  10 minutes 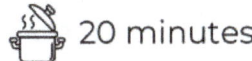 20 minutes

Ingredients

- 2 cups buttermilk baking mix
- 1 pound pork sausage
- 1 (11-ounce) can of condensed cream of Cheddar cheese soup

Preparation

- Set oven temperature to 350 degrees F. (175 degrees C).
- Baking mix, sausage, and cheddar cheese soup should all be mixed in a big basin.
- Combine all the ingredients and roll them into balls that are exactly 1 inch in diameter.
- For best results, pop the balls into the oven and let them bake for 15–20 minutes, or until a toothpick inserted in the centre comes out clean.

Seasoned Crackers

32 servings | 10 minutes | 15 minutes

Ingredients

- 1 (12-ounce) package of oyster crackers
- 1 (1 ounce) package of ranch dressing mix
- 1/2 teaspoon dried dill weed
- 1/4 teaspoon garlic powder
- 3/4 cup vegetable oil

Preparation

- Instruct the reader to set the oven temperature at 200 degrees F. (95 degrees C).
- Combine oil and seasonings in a bowl and whisk until smooth; pour over crackers and toss to coat.
- Toss all the ingredients together on a large baking sheet and bake for 20 minutes.
- After 10 minutes, stir the pan and keep it in the oven for another 10.

Spiced Pumpkin Dip

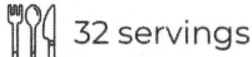 32 servings  15 minutes  15 minutes

Ingredients

- 1 (8-ounce) package of cream cheese, softened
- 2 cups confectioners' sugar
- 1 (15-ounce) can of pumpkin puree
- 1 tablespoon Pumpkin Pie Spice
- 1 teaspoon pure Orange Extract
- 1/2 teaspoon Ground Ginger
- gingersnap cookies

Preparation

- Cream cheese and powdered sugar should be blended in a food processor until completely smooth.
- Take the lid off, then mix in the pumpkin and the rest of the ingredients.
- Use a good amount of mixing time.
- Put in the fridge and chill for at least 30 minutes.
- Eat with gingersnaps.

Stuffed Jalapenos

 20 servings   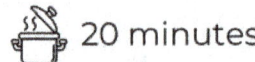 5 minutes   20 minutes

Ingredients

- 2 (7-ounce) cans of jalapeno peppers
- 6 ounces shredded Mexican-style cheese blend
- 1 pound pork sausage, hot
- 1 (5.5 ounces) package of spicy seasoning coating mix

Preparation

- How to make stuffed peppers: cut peppers in half lengthwise, remove the stem and seeds, and then stuff them with cheese.
- Make sausage links by rolling them out with a pin between two sheets of plastic wrap.
- The sausage should be unwrapped and a tiny slice wrapped around each jalapeno.
- A spicy seasoning blend is rolled into peppers.
- Bake for 15–25 minutes at 350°F (175°C) until golden and bubbling and the cheese is melted.

Stuffed Mushrooms II

 10 servings    25 minutes   15 minutes

Ingredients

- 1 pound fresh mushrooms, stems removed
- 1 (12-ounce) package of chicken-flavour stuffing mix
- 1 (10.75 ounces) can condense cream of mushroom soup
- 10 3/4 fluid ounces of milk

Preparation

- Turn oven temperature up to 350 degrees F. (175 degrees C). Prepare a 9-by-13-inch greased baking pan.
- Make filling as directed on the box.
- Stuff the mushrooms and arrange them in a baking tray.
- One can of milk to one can of soup. Put the liquid over the mushrooms, cover the dish, and bake for 25 minutes.

Sugar Coated Pecans

 12 servings  10 minutes 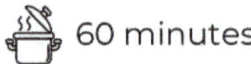 60 minutes

Ingredients

- 1 egg white
- 1 tablespoon water
- 1 pound pecan halves
- 1 cup white sugar
- 3/4 teaspoon salt
- 1/2 teaspoon ground cinnamon

Preparation

- Instruct the reader to set the oven temperature to 250 degrees F. (120 degrees C).
- Prepare one baking sheet by greasing it with butter.
- The egg white and water should be beaten together in a bowl until foamy.
- Sugar, salt, and cinnamon should be combined in a separate basin.
- Egg whites should be added to pecans, and the nuts should be stirred to get a uniform coating.
- Take out the nuts, then roll them around in the sugar solution to coat them.
- Toss the nuts on the baking sheet.
- For an hour, heat the oven to 250 degrees Fahrenheit (120 degrees C).
- To prevent burning, stir the mixture every 15 minutes.

Sweet Pickled Eggs

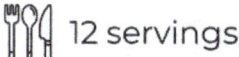 12 servings  10 minutes 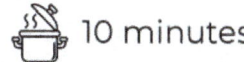 10 minutes

Ingredients

- 12 eggs
- 1 large onion, sliced into rings
- 2 cups white wine vinegar
- 2 cups water
- 1/2 cup white sugar
- 1 teaspoon salt
- 1 tablespoon pickling spice, wrapped in cheesecloth

Preparation

- Instructions: Fill a big kettle with water to cover the eggs.
- Use a lid to keep the contents inside. Do so over medium heat until it reaches a boil.
- Ten minutes at a low boil.
- Drain. To cool eggs, rinse them in cold water. eggs in a shell
- In a saucepan, combine the vinegar, water, sugar, and salt to make the brine.
- Be sure the sugar is dissolved by stirring it over a medium flame.
- In a clean 2-litre jar, stack the entire eggs and onion rings until they reach within an inch of the top.

Sweet Pickled Eggs

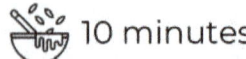 12 servings 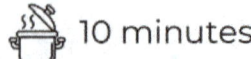 10 minutes 10 minutes

Preparation

- To the brine, add the pickling spices.
- The bag must be agitated for a full 30 seconds.
- Put away the bag.
- Cover the eggs with brine up to about a quarter of an inch from the top of the jar.
- Put a clean lid on it and screw it on tight.
- Keep for a week or two in the fridge before serving.
- To be served cold.

Sweet Potato Balls

8 servings 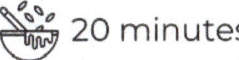 20 minutes  20 minutes

Ingredients

- 1 (40-ounce) can of sweet potatoes, drained
- 1/4 cup butter
- salt to taste
- 3 cups crushed cornflakes cereal
- 3/4 cup real maple syrup
- 10 large marshmallows

Preparation

- To prepare the sweet potatoes as directed, drain them and place them in a large mixing basin.
- Put some butter or margarine in the mashed potatoes.
- Use salt as desired.
- Roll the dough into balls about three inches in diameter.
- Sprinkle with cornflakes and place in a greased 9-by-12-inch baking dish.
- Coat the balls thoroughly with maple syrup.
- Put in the oven and cook for 40 minutes at 325 degrees F (165 degrees C).
- Within the final fifteen minutes, a marshmallow was placed on top of each ball.

Tasty Toothpick Appetizers

20 servings  10 minutes  10 minutes

Ingredients

- toothpicks
- 1/2 pound fully cooked kielbasa or Polish sausage, cut into 1/2-inch pieces
- 1 (10 ounces) jar of red or green maraschino cherries, drained
- 1 (5-ounce) jar of small green olives
- 1 (8-ounce) package of processed cheese food, cubed

Preparation

- Here's what you need to do: thread a sausage slice, a cherry, an olive, and a cheese cube onto a toothpick.
- Set them out in a tidy pile on a dish.
- The toothpick's contents should be consumed all at once, but the toothpick itself should be avoided.

Thanksgiving Cheese Ball

 8 servings    15 minutes   240 minutes

Ingredients

- 8 ounces of cream cheese
- 4 ounces sharp Cheddar cheese
- 2 ounces of crumbled blue cheese
- 2 tablespoons grated onion
- 1 clove garlic, minced
- 4 dashes of Worcestershire sauce
- 1 (2.25 ounce) can of green olives
- 1/2 cup chopped pecans

Thanksgiving Cheese Ball

 8 servings   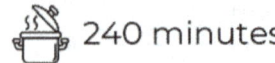 15 minutes   240 minutes

Preparation

- Combine the cream cheese, Cheddar cheese, blue cheese, onion, garlic, and Worcestershire sauce in a food processor and blend until smooth.
- Do not stop processing until everything is well combined. Put in some olives and chop them up in a food processor.
- Roll a ball of the mixture in the chopped pecans to coat.
- Refrigerate for at least four hours after being wrapped in plastic.

Thanksgiving Won-Tons

 20 servings    30 minutes   15 minutes

Ingredients

- 1 1/2 cups cooked turkey breast meat, shredded
- 2/3 cup dried cranberries
- 1/3 cup slivered almonds
- 1/2 cup cranberry sauce
- 1 (14-ounce) package of wonton wrappers
- 1-quart vegetable oil for frying

Preparation

- Put the turkey, cranberries, almonds, and cranberry sauce in a bowl and mix well.
- Fill the middle of each wonton wrapper with roughly a spoonful of the filling.
- Wrappers should be pressed with a fork to seal after being folded over the filling and moistened.
- Prepare the oil in a deep fryer or large skillet.
- Golden brown wontons can be achieved by frying them in hot oil. Pour the waste into some paper towels.

Turkey Dumplings

 10 servings  15 minutes 45 minutes

Ingredients

- 1 pound cooked, chopped turkey meat
- 3 cups water
- salt and pepper to taste
- 3 tablespoons all-purpose flour
- 1 (12-ounce) package of refrigerated biscuit dough

Preparation

- In a medium saucepan, bring the turkey, water, salt, and pepper to a boil.
- Turn down the heat and let the broth form over 30–40 minutes.
- Coat a medium-sized chopping board or another flat surface with flour.
- To make biscuits, roll out the dough and slice it into squares that are 1x2 inches.
- Just toss the pieces into the stock and simmer for around 15 minutes.

Vegetable Dip

 12 servings  5 minutes 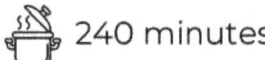 240 minutes

Ingredients

- 1 cup mayonnaise
- 1 teaspoon curry powder
- 1 teaspoon crushed garlic
- 3 teaspoons tarragon vinegar
- 1 teaspoon grated onion
- 1 teaspoon prepared horseradish

Preparation

- For the dressing, whisk together the mayonnaise, curry powder, garlic, vinegar, onion, and horseradish in a separate small bowl.
- Combine, cover, and refrigerate the mixture overnight.

Apple Orchard Punch

 12 servings 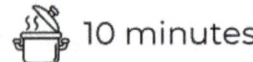 10 minutes 10 minutes

Ingredients

- 1 (32 fluid ounce) bottle of apple juice, chilled
- 1 (12 fluid ounce) can freeze cranberry juice concentrate
- 1 cup orange juice
- 1 1/2 litres ginger ale
- 1 apple

Preparation

- TO MAKE: Combine apple juice, cranberry juice concentrate, and orange juice in a big punch bowl.
- Slowly pour in the ginger ale while continuing to stir until the sugar has dissolved.
- Using a sharp knife, carefully slice the apple vertically into paper-thin discs.
- Apple slices can be floated on top of the punch.

Apple Pie

 8 servings    30 minutes    45 minutes

Ingredients

- 1-gallon apple juice
- 1-gallon apple cider
- 3 cups white sugar
- 8 cinnamon sticks
- 1 (750 milliliters) bottle 190 proof grain alcohol

Preparation

- The recipe calls for apple juice, apple cider, sugar, and cinnamon sticks to be combined in a big pot.
- Achieve a rolling boil, then turn off the heat and set aside to cool.
- Stir in the grain alcohol once the juice mixture has cooled.

Cherry Cider

6 servings  10 minutes 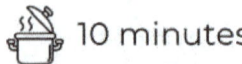 10 minutes

Ingredients

- 2 quarts apple cider
- 1 (3-inch) cinnamon stick
- 1 (3-ounce) package of cherry gelatin

Preparation

- Follow these simple steps: in a saucepan, bring the cider and cinnamon stick to a boil.
- Simmer for 15 minutes at low heat. Cook the gelatin for 2 minutes, stirring regularly, or until it has completely dissolved. Make sure it's served hot.

Coffee Liqueur

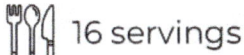 16 servings  5 minutes  10 minutes

Ingredients

- 4 cups white sugar
- 4 cups water
- 3/4 cup instant coffee granules
- 2 tablespoons vanilla extract
- 4 cups vodka

Preparation

- TO MAKE: Mix the sugar and water in a three-quart saucepan and cook on medium.
- Simmer for 10 minutes after bringing to a boil.
- Turn off the heat and add the instant coffee while stirring.
- To the cooled mixture, add the vanilla essence and vodka.
- Empty into sterile containers.
- Keep bottles sealed and store them in the fridge or a dark cupboard.

Cranberry Pineapple Juice

 14 servings    5 minutes   5 minutes

Ingredients

- 1 (64 fluid ounce) bottle of cranberry juice, chilled
- 1 (46 fluid ounce) can of pineapple juice
- 1 (8-ounce) can of pineapple tidbits
- 1 cup cranberries

Preparation

- Combine the cranberry juice and pineapple juice in a large punch bowl.
- Add in pineapple chunks and cranberries and mix well. Use ice if serving.

Cranberry Punch

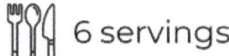 6 servings    5 minutes    5 minutes

Ingredients

- 1 1/2 litres cranberry-apple juice
- 1-litre ginger ale
- 2 limes, thinly sliced
- 6 sprigs of fresh mint
- 6 cups ice

Preparation

- The instructions here are to fill six tall glasses halfway with ice.
- You can use a mixture of cranberry and apple juice to fill it up to around two-thirds.
- Divide the ginger ale among the glasses.
- The ingredients need only be gently stirred. Accent with lime wedges and mint leaves.

Cranberry Tea

 14 servings   15 minutes   90 minutes

Ingredients

- 3 teaspoons instant tea powder
- 1/2 teaspoon ground allspice
- 1/2 teaspoon ground cinnamon
- 1/2 teaspoon ground nutmeg
- 6 cups boiling water
- 1 (3-ounce) package cherry flavoured gelatin
- 1 cup orange juice
- 1/4 cup lemon juice
- 1-quart cranberry juice
- 1/2 cup white sugar

Preparation

- Use a tea bag to soak the instant tea, allspice, cinnamon, and nutmeg in boiling water for 5 minutes. Let the cherry gelatin cool before stirring it in.
- Combine the sugar, lemon juice, orange juice, and cranberry juice.
- Until the sugar is completely dissolved, mix.
- Serve hot and store leftovers in the fridge.

Eggnog Extreme

 20 servings   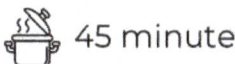 45 minutes   45 minutes

Ingredients

- 1 (64 fluid ounce) bottle of apple cider
- 3 cinnamon sticks
- 1 teaspoon whole allspice
- 1 teaspoon whole cloves
- 1/3 cup brown sugar

Preparation

- Place apple cider and cinnamon sticks in a slow cooker.
- Put some cloves and allspice in a little cheesecloth and throw that in the pot.
- Blend with some brown sugar.
- Toss into a pot and turn the heat up high to where it will boil.
- Turn down the thermostat and bundle up.

Eggnog I

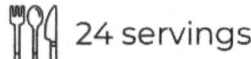 24 servings  15 minutes  15 minutes

Ingredients

- 2 egg yolks
- 1/4 cup white sugar
- 1 pinch salt
- 2 cups milk
- 2 tablespoons rum
- 1/2 cup heavy whipping cream
- 1 pinch of ground nutmeg

Preparation

- In the top of a double boiler, combine the egg yolks, sugar, and salt and whisk until smooth.
- Integrate the milk and stir until smooth.
- Cook the mixture over a pot of boiling water, stirring constantly, until it thickens enough to coat a metal spoon.
- Pour in the rum, and set it in the fridge.
- Whisk the heavy cream until stiff peaks form.
- Mix in the grated nutmeg and then fold in the cooled egg mixture.

Eggnog II

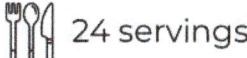 24 servings  15 minutes  15 minutes

Ingredients

- 6 eggs, beaten
- 2 1/4 cups milk
- 1/3 cup white sugar
- 1 teaspoon vanilla extract
- 1 cup heavy whipping cream
- 2 teaspoons white sugar
- 1 pinch of ground nutmeg

Preparation

- Put the eggs, milk, and a third of a cup of sugar in a large pot and whisk to mix.
- Stir the mixture constantly over medium heat until it coats the back of a spoon.
- Take it away from the heat.
- Set the pan in a sink or bowl of ice water and stir occasionally for 1 to 2 minutes to swiftly cool the contents of the pan.
- Mix in the vanilla extract.
- Allow chilling for 4 to 24 hours.
- Soft peaks should form after whipping the cream with the 2 teaspoons of sugar right before serving.
- Place the egg mixture in a punch bowl in the refrigerator.
- Mix in the whipped topping, and serve immediately.
- Use nutmeg as a garnish for each serving.

Holiday Punch I

 32 servings   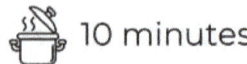 10 minutes   10 minutes

Ingredients

- 1 13-Pound WHOLE 4 cups cranberry juice cocktail
- 8 cups prepared lemonade
- 2 cups orange juice
- 1 (4 ounces) jar maraschino cherries
- 1 (2 litres) bottle of ginger ale
- 1 orange, sliced in rounds

Preparation

- In a large punch bowl, mix cranberry juice cocktail, lemonade, and orange juice.
- Toss in some maraschino cherries and mix well. Keep cold for at least two hours.
- Add the ginger ale right before serving.
- Add an orange slice to the rim of each glass.

Hot Buttered Rum Batter

🍴 10 servings   🥣 10 minutes   🍲 10 minutes

Ingredients

- 1 pound butter
- 1 pound brown sugar
- 1 pound confectioners' sugar
- 1-quart vanilla ice cream softened
- 1 tablespoon ground cinnamon
- 1 teaspoon ground nutmeg

Preparation

- To follow these instructions, melt butter in a big pot over medium heat.
- Combine brown sugar and powdered sugar.
- Toss in the ice cream, cinnamon, and nutmeg after the pot has been taken off the heat.
- Combine ingredients, then transfer them to a freezer-safe plastic container.
- One spoonful of Hot Buttered Rum Batter and one ounce of rum should be combined with hot water in a coffee mug. Nutmeg should be sprinkled on top of the drink and stirred before serving.

Pumpkin Pie Smoothie

 1 servings  5 minutes 5 minutes

Ingredients

- 1 (15 ounces) can solid pack pumpkin puree
- 1 (12 fluid ounce) can freeze apple juice concentrate
- 1/8 teaspoon ground nutmeg
- 1 teaspoon ground cinnamon
- 2 1/2 cups water

Preparation

- To follow the instructions, drain the pumpkin and place it in the freezer for an hour.
- Blend up some frozen pumpkin, some apple juice concentrate, some nutmeg, and some cinnamon. Mix it up until it's a homogenous paste.
- Even as you fill the blender with water, keep blending.

Warm and Spicy Autumn Punch

 16 servings   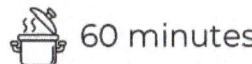 20 minutes   60 minutes

Ingredients

- 2 oranges
- 8 whole cloves
- 6 cups apple juice
- 1 cinnamon stick
- 1/4 teaspoon ground nutmeg
- 1/4 cup honey
- 3 tablespoons lemon juice
- 2 1/4 cups pineapple juice

Preparation

- To prepare, set the oven temperature to 350 degrees F. (175 degrees C). Bake the oranges for 30 minutes with cloves inserted into their flesh.
- Add the apple juice and cinnamon stick to a large pot.
- Then, reduce the heat to medium and simmer for 5 minutes.
- Take off the stove and add the honey, lemon juice, pineapple juice, and nutmeg.
- Float two cooked oranges stuffed with cloves on the hot punch and serve in a large bowl.

Brown Bread

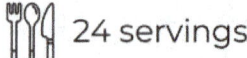 24 servings   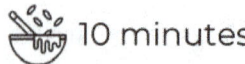 10 minutes   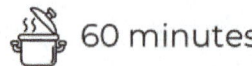 60 minutes

Ingredients

- 2 cups milk
- 1/2 cup white sugar
- 1/2 cup molasses
- 1 1/2 cups whole wheat flour
- 1 1/2 cups bread flour
- 1/2 teaspoon salt
- 1 teaspoon baking soda
- 3 teaspoons baking powder

Preparation

- Please prepare two 9-by-5-inch bread pans as directed. Set oven temperature to 350 degrees F. (175 degrees C).
- Mix the milk, sugar, and molasses in a little bowl.
- Blend white flour, whole wheat flour, salt, baking soda, and baking powder.
- Combine this with the milk and stir until well incorporated.
- Put the batter into the bread pans.
- Put something in the oven and wait 45 minutes.

Banana Cranberry Bread

 12 servings   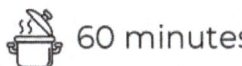 15 minutes   60 minutes

Ingredients

- 2 1/2 cups white sugar
- 1 cup shortening
- 3 eggs
- 3 mashed bananas
- 1 cup cranberry sauce
- 1/2 cup milk
- 1 teaspoon vanilla extract
- 4 cups all-purpose flour
- 1 1/2 teaspoons baking soda
- 1 1/2 teaspoons baking powder
- 1 teaspoon ground cinnamon
- 1/2 teaspoon ground nutmeg
- 1/2 cup chopped walnuts

Banana Cranberry Bread

 12 servings 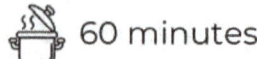 15 minutes 60 minutes

Preparation

- To prepare, set the oven temperature to 350 degrees F. (175 degrees C). Prepare two 9-by-5-inch loaf pans with butter.
- Sugar and shortening should be creamed together in a large bowl until frothy.
- Bananas, cranberry sauce, milk, vanilla extract, and eggs should all be mixed and then beaten.
- Sift together the flour, baking soda, baking powder, cinnamon, and nutmeg in a separate basin.
- Combine the flour and bananas gradually.
- Mix in the chopped walnuts.
- Toss into the greased loaf pans.
- A toothpick inserted in the centre should come out clean after 50-60 minutes in the preheated oven. After letting them rest in the pan for 10 minutes, flip them out onto a wire rack to finish cooling.

Best Ever Banana Bread

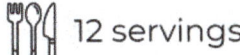 12 servings  15 minutes  60 minutes

Ingredients

- 2 eggs, beaten
- 1/3 cup buttermilk
- 1/2 cup vegetable oil
- 1 cup mashed bananas
- 1 1/2 cups white sugar
- 1 3/4 cups all-purpose flour
- 1 teaspoon baking soda
- 1/2 teaspoon salt
- 1/2 cup chopped pecans (optional)

Preparation

- Set oven temperature to 325 degrees F. (165 degrees C). Use non-stick cooking spray to coat one 9x5-inch loaf pan.
- Using a blender, combine the eggs, buttermilk, oil, and bananas.
- Mix the baking powder, salt, and sugar into the flour.
- Mix the pecans with the banana mixture.
- Combine everything thoroughly.
- Bake for 1 hour and 20 minutes, or until a cake tester inserted in the centre comes out clean, after pouring into the prepared loaf pan.

Country Banana Bread

 12 servings   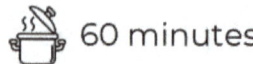 15 minutes   60 minutes

Ingredients

- 1 (18.25 ounce) package of yellow cake mix
- 3 eggs
- 1 1/3 cups vegetable oil
- 4 bananas, mashed

Preparation

- To prepare, set the oven temperature to 350 degrees F. (175 degrees C). Prepare a 9x13-inch greased pan.
- Cake mix, eggs, oil, and bananas should all be combined in one basin.
- Put the contents of the bowl into the pan.
- Cook for 35-40 minutes in an oven warmed to 350 degrees Fahrenheit (175 degrees Celsius).

Cranberry Muffins

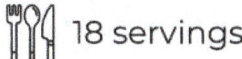 18 servings  15 minutes  20 minutes

Ingredients

- 2 cups all-purpose flour
- 1 cup white sugar
- 1 1/2 teaspoons baking powder
- 1/2 teaspoon baking soda
- 2 teaspoons orange zest
- 1 1/2 teaspoons ground nutmeg
- 1 teaspoon ground cinnamon
- 1/2 teaspoon ground ginger
- 1/2 cup shortening
- 3/4 cup orange juice
- 1 teaspoon vanilla extract
- 2 eggs, beaten
- 1 1/2 cups chopped cranberries
- 1 1/2 cups chopped walnuts
- 1 (8-ounce) can of whole cranberry sauce
- 2 tablespoons brown sugar, packed
- 1/4 cup margarine

Cranberry Muffins

18 servings  15 minutes 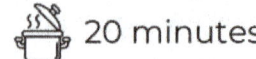 20 minutes

Preparation

- Set oven temperature to 350 degrees F. (175 degrees C).
- Prepare a muffin pan with 12 cups and another with 6 cups by spraying it with cooking spray or by greasing it.
- Combine the dry ingredients (flour, sugar, baking powder, baking soda) with the wet (orange peel, nutmeg, cinnamon, and ginger).
- Toss in some cranberries, some nuts, some vanilla extract, some orange juice, and some shortening.
- Bake for 25 minutes, or until the tops are golden, in muffin tins.
- To make the topping, combine the cranberry sauce, brown sugar, and margarine in a skillet and stir over low heat until smooth.
- Warm-up and smooth out in the oven. Take it off the heat and spread it on the muffins.

Cranberry Nut Bread I

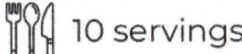 10 servings  10 minutes  50 minutes

Ingredients

- 2 cups all-purpose flour
- 3/4 cup white sugar
- 3/4 teaspoon salt
- 1 1/2 teaspoons baking powder
- 1/2 teaspoon baking soda
- 1 cup chopped cranberries
- 1/2 cup chopped walnuts
- 1 egg
- 2 tablespoons vegetable oil
- 3/4 cup orange juice
- 1 tablespoon orange zest

Preparation

- To prepare, set the oven temperature to 350 degrees F. (175 degrees C). The loaf pan, measuring 9 by 5, should be greased.
- Stir together the flour, sugar, salt, baking powder, and baking soda.
- Stir in the flour until the cranberries and walnuts are evenly coated.
- Combine the egg with the oil, orange juice, orange zest, and orange zest.
- Add the egg mixture to the flour and whisk until everything is just combined.
- Drop the batter by spoonfuls into the pan.
- Bake in the preheated oven for 50 minutes, or until a toothpick inserted close to the centre comes out clean. Ten minutes is enough time to cool in the pan before transferring it to a wire rack to finish cooling.

Cranberry Nut Bread II

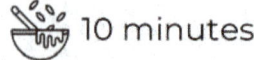 10 servings 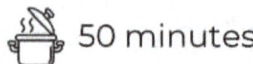 10 minutes 50 minutes

Ingredients

- 2 cups all-purpose flour
- 1 cup white sugar
- 1 1/2 teaspoons baking powder
- 1 teaspoon salt
- 1/2 teaspoon baking soda
- 1/4 cup butter
- 1 egg
- 3/4 cup orange juice
- 1 tablespoon grated orange zest
- 1 1/2 cups fresh or frozen cranberries
- 1/2 cup chopped walnuts

Preparation

- To prepare, set the oven temperature to 350 degrees F. (175 degrees C).
- An 8-by-4-inch loaf pan should be lightly greased.
- Combine the dry ingredients (flour, sugar, baking powder, salt, and baking soda) in a medium bowl.
- The mixture should resemble coarse crumbs once the butter has been cut in.
- Combine the egg, orange juice, and orange zest in a small bowl and beat until combined.
- Add to the dry ingredients and combine.
- Blend in the cranberries and the walnuts.
- Put into a loaf pan.
- To test doneness, stick a wooden toothpick into the centre of the cake and remove it cleanly. Bake in the preheated oven for 65–70 minutes.
- Remove from pan after 10 minutes and let cool completely on a wire rack.

Date and Nut Bread

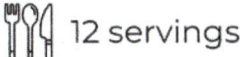 12 servings  20 minutes 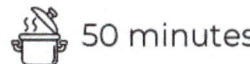 50 minutes

Ingredients

- 1 1/2 cups hot water
- 1 1/2 cups dates, pitted and chopped
- 2 teaspoons baking soda
- 1 cup white sugar
- 1 teaspoon salt
- 1 tablespoon butter, melted
- 1 egg
- 1 teaspoon vanilla extract
- 1 cup chopped walnuts
- 2 3/4 cups all-purpose flour

Preparation

- To prepare, set the oven temperature to 350 degrees F. (175 degrees C). Preparation of a greased loaf pan.
- When the water has cooled, pour it over the dates.
- Combine the flour, baking soda, sugar, and salt in a large sifter.
- Blend in the ice water and cooled dates.
- To the melted butter, egg, vanilla, and walnuts, add the other ingredients.
- Combine everything thoroughly. The batter is ready; pour it into the dish.
- Bake until a toothpick inserted near the middle comes out clean, about 1 hour at 350 degrees F (175 degrees C).
- In ten minutes, remove the bread from the pan. Take the bread out of the pan and place it on a cooling rack.

Grandmother's Famous Cranberry Bread

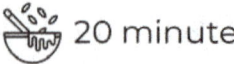 12 servings   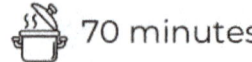 20 minutes   70 minutes

Ingredients

- 2 cups sifted all-purpose flour
- 1 cup white sugar
- 1 1/2 teaspoons baking powder
- 1 teaspoon salt
- 1/2 teaspoon baking soda
- 1/4 cup butter
- 1 egg, beaten
- 1 teaspoon orange zest
- 3/4 cup orange juice
- 1 1/2 cups golden raisins
- 1 1/2 cups chopped cranberries

Preparation

- Set oven temperature to 350 degrees F. (175 degrees C).
- Prepare one loaf pan that measures 9 by 5 by 3 inches by spraying it with cooking spray or by greasing it.
- The flour, sugar, baking powder, salt, and baking soda should be whisked together.
- To make a crumbly mixture, cut in butter.
- Mix in the egg, orange peel, and orange juice, and then fold in the dried fruit.
- Make sure a toothpick inserted in the centre comes out clean before removing the bread from the oven.
- Take out of the oven and let cool on a wire rack.

Knodel

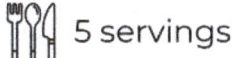 5 servings    15 minutes    160 minutes

Ingredients

- 1 onion, chopped
- 2 tablespoons chopped fresh parsley
- 2 teaspoons butter
- 1/2 (1 pound) loaf of white bread, toasted and cut into cubes
- 2 eggs, beaten
- 1 cup milk
- salt and pepper to taste

Preparation

- For one 9-by-11-inch baking dish, butter it thoroughly.
- Mix the onion, parsley, and butter in a skillet and heat it over medium heat.
- Brown the onions in the cooking process.
- Toss the bread pieces with the dressing after pouring it over them.
- Combine the eggs, milk, salt, and pepper in a bowl with a whisk.
- Blend into the onion and bread crumbs and let sit for an hour.
- Compact the mixture into the baking dish, and then cover it securely with aluminium foil.

Knodel

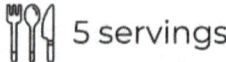 5 servings  15 minutes  160 minutes

Preparation

- Put the baking dish on a rack inside a larger pot and fill the larger pot with water until it reaches about 3 inches above the baking dish.
- Prepare by covering and steaming for an hour.
- Take out of the heat and let sit for 10 minutes.
- Before serving, drizzle with melted butter.

Apple Cranberry Pie

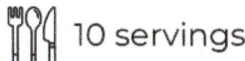 10 servings 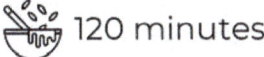 120 minutes  65 minutes

Ingredients

- 1 (15-ounce) package of refrigerated piecrusts
- 1/2 cup Calorie Sweetener, Granular
- 1 tablespoon all-purpose flour
- 1/2 teaspoon ground cinnamon
- 4 large Granny Smith apples - peeled, cored and sliced
- 1 cup cranberries, coarsely chopped

Preparation

- TAKE ONE PIE Crust OUT OF THE FOLDS AND PRESS OUT THE FOLD LINES.
- The pie crust should be prepared and placed on a 9-inch pie plate as instructed on the packaging.
- COMBINE Toss the apples and cranberries with the granular, flour, and cinnamon in a large basin. Fill the pie crust with the ingredients.
- Flatten out the leftover pie crust by unfolding it.
- A thickness of 1/8 inch is the target.
- Position overfilling, then tuck in and crimp the edges.
- Vent the steam by cutting holes at the top.
- BAKE for 40–50 minutes, until the crust is brown.
- Wrap the edges in aluminium foil to keep them from burning.
- A one-hour cooling period on a wire rack is required before serving.

Cranberry Apple Pie I

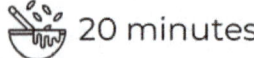 8 servings    20 minutes   45 minutes

Ingredients

- 1 (9-inch) deep dish pie crust
- 6 apples - peeled, cored and chopped
- 1 (12-ounce) package of fresh cranberries, roughly chopped
- 1 1/2 cups white sugar
- 1/3 cup quick-cooking tapioca
- 1 1/2 cups all-purpose flour
- 3/4 cup packed brown sugar
- 1 teaspoon ground cinnamon
- 1/2 teaspoon salt
- 2/3 cup unsalted butter
- 1 egg, lightly beaten

Preparation

- Set oven temperature to 325 degrees F. (165 degrees C).
- Turn the pie shell upside down over a second, similar pan. The crust won't recede into the pan if you do this.
- For 10 minutes, this is how you'll bake until you've got some crust. Flip the crust over and take out the second pie dish from inside.
- Apples, cranberries, and sugar should be mixed in a big basin. Set aside for 20 minutes while covered.

Cranberry Apple Pie I

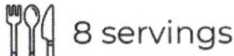 8 servings  20 minutes  45 minutes

Preparation

- On to the fruit juice, add the tapioca and let it sit for 15 to 20 minutes. Fill the partially baked pie crust with the ingredients.
- Flour, brown sugar, cinnamon, salt, and butter should all be mixed in a medium bowl. Use your fingers to knead the ingredients together until a crumbly texture forms. Use it to cover the apple-cranberry filling. Use an egg that has been lightly beaten to paint the pastry crust.
- The pie should be set on a cookie sheet to prevent any spills. In a preheated oven, place the apples on the bottom shelf and bake for 45-60 minutes, checking on them every 15 minutes.

Cranberry Apple Pie II

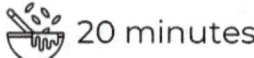 8 servings    20 minutes   45 minutes

Ingredients

- 6 apples
- 1 (16-ounce) can of whole cranberry sauce
- 1/2 cup packed brown sugar
- 1/3 cup all-purpose flour
- 1 1/2 teaspoons ground cinnamon
- 1/2 teaspoon ground nutmeg
- 1 recipe pastry for a 9-inch double-crust pie

Preparation

- Set oven temperature to 350 degrees F. (175 degrees C). Pastry-line a pie dish.
- Make apple slices after peeling, coring, and slicing the apples.
- Squish the cranberry sauce and apples together in a bowl. Add the apples to the combination of brown sugar, flour, cinnamon, and nutmeg. Combine in complete blending. Put the filling into the pastry-lined pan. Put on a crusty topping. Finish up with a crimp. Dot the top crust with cuts.
- For a golden crust and bubbling filling, bake for 1 hour.

Cranberry Pecan Pie

 8 servings  25 minutes 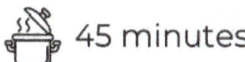 45 minutes

Ingredients

- 1 (9-inch) deep dish pie crust
- 1 cup cranberries
- 3 eggs
- 2/3 cup white sugar
- 1 cup dark corn syrup
- 6 tablespoons unsalted butter, melted
- 1 teaspoon vanilla extract
- 1/4 teaspoon ground mace
- 1/8 teaspoon salt
- 1 cup pecan halves

Preparation

- To prepare, set the oven temperature to 350 degrees F. (175 degrees C).
- Cranberries should be finely chopped, either in a food processor or by hand. In a pie pan lined with crust, spread the filling to cover the bottom.
- Whip eggs in a big bowl until they foam. Then, stir in the sugar, corn syrup, melted butter or margarine, vanilla, mace, and salt. Combine everything thoroughly. Pour the mixture over the cranberry layer. Place pecan halves cut side up, on top of the sugar.
- For 45-50 minutes in a preheated oven, until brown and firm in the middle.

Cranberry Pie I

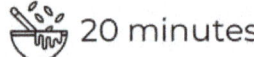 6 servings    20 minutes   45 minutes

Ingredients

- 1 recipe pastry for a 9-inch double-crust pie
- 3 cups cranberries
- 1 cup raisins
- 2 tablespoons all-purpose flour
- 1 1/4 cups white sugar
- 1/2 cup water
- 1 teaspoon vanilla extract

Preparation

- Set oven temperature to 450 degrees F. (230 degrees C). Use the crust to line a 9-inch pie pan; set aside the excess to use as the pie's topping.
- Put both in the fridge while you prepare the filling.
- Roughly chop the cranberries. Combine with raisins, flour, sugar, water, and vanilla.
- Fill a refrigerated pie shell. There on the top crust, cut slashes in it, and crimp the edges so they stay put.
- Put in a hot oven and wait 10 minutes. Bake for a further 30 minutes at 350 degrees F (175 degrees C). Let cool before serving.

Honey Baked Apples

2 servings  20 minutes  30 minutes

Ingredients

- 6 green apples
- 1 1/2 cups fresh cranberries
- 2 1/4 cups water
- 3/4 cup packed brown sugar
- 3 tablespoons honey
- 6 scoops vanilla ice cream

Preparation

- Set oven temperature to 350 degrees F. (175 degrees C).
- Take a corner of the apples and peel off the top third of the fruit. Put them in a casserole and stuff as many cranberries as you can into the cavities left by the cores.
- In the meantime, in a small saucepan, mix the brown sugar, honey, and water until the sugar has dissolved. To dissolve the sugar and honey, bring to a boil and whisk occasionally. Pour the hot liquid over the apples after it has come to a boil.
- Baste every 15 to 20 minutes while baking for 1 hour in a preheated oven. Add vanilla ice cream and serve.

Mincemeat II

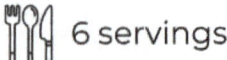 6 servings   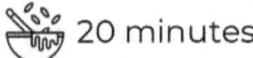 20 minutes    30 minutes

Ingredients

- 3 pounds pork butt roast
- 2 (12-ounce) packages of fresh cranberries
- 3 cups water
- 1 quart chopped apples
- 1 large orange
- 1 lemon
- 2 pounds raisins
- 3 (16 ounces) cans of pitted sour red pie cherries
- 3 (16 ounces) cans of gooseberries
- 2 cups brandy
- 2 cups distilled white vinegar
- 4 cups white sugar
- 1 tablespoon ground cloves
- 1 tablespoon ground nutmeg
- 2 tablespoons ground cinnamon
- 2 tablespoons ground allspice

Mincemeat II

 6 servings   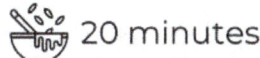 20 minutes    30 minutes

Preparation

- To prepare, set the oven temperature to 350 degrees F. (175 degrees C). Put the meat in a roasting pan and cook it for about 1 1/2 hours, or until it reaches the desired tenderness. When meat is done, take it out but leave the oven on.
- Cranberries can be cooked in a medium saucepan with water while the meat is in the oven. Simmer on low heat until cranberries begin to burst.
- Upon completion of the beef, grind it with the chopped apples, and set aside.
- Put the orange and lemon peels that you've been grinding down in a big baking dish. Combine sugar, brandy, vinegar, cranberries, raisins, cherries, gooseberries, cinnamon, nutmeg, cloves, and allspice. Mix everything and add to the meat.
- Place the aluminium foil-covered pan in the oven. Mincemeat needs to be heated for 30 minutes with stirring.
- Prepare a sufficient quantity of sterilised canning jars and matching lids to store all of the mincemeat.
- Prepare a big stockpot by placing a wire rack in the bottom and filling it with water to the halfway point. Crank up the heat and get the water boiling.

Mincemeat II

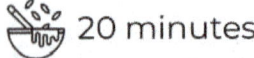 6 servings    20 minutes   30 minutes

Preparation

- Make sure there are no voids or air bubbles in the mincemeat before packing it into the sterilised jars. Pack containers to the brim, then secure the tops. Carefully place the jars into the hot water using the holder. Place at least 2 inches of space between each jar. If the jars aren't covered by at least two inches of water, add extra boiling water. Put in the 30 minutes of covered processing time.
- A holder can be used to safely remove the jars from the water, and then they can be placed on a wooden or cloth-covered surface, spaced out by at least 2 inches. Once the jar has cooled, press down on the lid to ensure a tight seal. A properly sealed lid can't rise or fall. It's recommended to let mincemeat sit for at least two months, preferably three, before using.

Baked Ziti with Turkey Meatballs

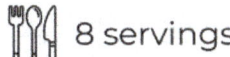 8 servings  20 minutes  120 minutes

Ingredients

- 1 pound ground turkey
- 1 clove garlic, minced
- 3/4 cup fresh bread crumbs
- 1/2 cup finely diced onion
- 3 tablespoons chopped, toasted pine nuts
- 1/2 cup chopped fresh parsley
- 1 egg, lightly beaten
- 1 teaspoon salt
- 1 teaspoon ground black pepper
- 4 tablespoons olive oil
- 1 (16-ounce) package of ziti pasta
- 1 1/2 cups mozzarella cheese, shredded
- 1 cup grated Romano cheese
- 6 cups tomato sauce
- 1-pint part-skim ricotta cheese

Baked Ziti with Turkey Meatballs

8 servings 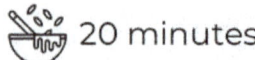 20 minutes 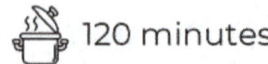 120 minutes

Preparation

- Add the turkey, garlic, bread crumbs, onion, pine nuts, parsley, egg, salt, and pepper to a bowl and mix well. Roll the ground beef into balls approximately an inch in diameter.
- Heat 2 tablespoons of oil in a big, heavy skillet over moderate heat until it is hot but not smoking. Shake the pan occasionally and cook the meatballs for about 4 minutes, or until they are browned and cooked through. Throw the meatballs on some paper towels to soak up any excess liquid. Toss the remaining meatballs into the pan with the 2 tablespoons of oil and brown them all.
- Turn oven temperature up to 375 degrees F. (190 degrees C). Prepare a gratin dish of 3 to 4 quarts capacity and oil it.
- Put some salt into a large kettle of water and get it boiling. Cook the pasta for 8 minutes, or until it is just al dente. Drain.

Baked Ziti with Turkey Meatballs

 8 servings  20 minutes 120 minutes

Preparation

- Combine the mozzarella and Romano in a small bowl.
- Place half the spaghetti in the bottom of the prepared dish, then add 1 1/2 cups of the tomato sauce and half the meatballs.
- Cover spaghetti with half of the remaining sauce and cheese mixture. Dollop the remaining ricotta cheese and meatballs on top.
- Cover the ricotta with the remaining spaghetti, then cover that with the sauce and cheese. For 30–35 minutes in the centre of the oven, or until golden. Reserve 10 minutes before serving.

Cranberry Stuffed Turkey Breasts

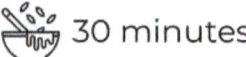 6 servings  30 minutes 120 minutes

Ingredients

- 2 boneless and skinless turkey breasts
- 1 (12-ounce) package herb-seasoned dry bread stuffing mix
- 1 1/2 cups sweetened-dried cranberries
- 1 cup chopped pecans
- 1/2 cup pecan halves
- 2 tablespoons olive oil

Preparation

- To Prepare stuffing mix as directed on the package; leave aside to cool.
- To lay flat, butterfly breasts can be opened with a sharp knife (this usually takes 3 cuts, depending on the size of the breasts).
- Use a mallet to pound each breast flat between two pieces of waxed paper.
- Spread stuffing to within a quarter inch of the edge of each breast. Coat with the remaining dried cranberries and the chopped pecans.
- Jelly-roll-style, beginning at the long end and rolling tightly to enclose the contents.
- Roll it up, tucking the ends in, and secure it with string at roughly 4-inch intervals along the length and once around the circumference.

Cranberry Stuffed Turkey Breasts

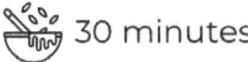 6 servings  30 minutes 120 minutes

Preparation

- Start by preheating the oven and then heating the olive oil in a skillet that can go in the oven.
- Be sure to brown the rolls evenly on all sides. Cover the skillet and bake it in an oven warmed to 350 degrees F (175 degrees C) for 1 hour, or until a knife inserted in the centre comes out clean. Keep an eye on the moisture level to ensure these don't dry out.
- After 15 minutes, slice the rolls into 1/2 to 3/4 inch rounds (remembering to remove the strings first). For a more impressive presentation, slice one bun but leave the other whole.
- The meat will have stuffing twisted into it.
- Place a bed of crinkled lettuce on your most decorative serving tray and top it with whole pecans and dried cranberries.

Pumpkin Stew

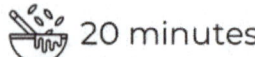 6 servings    20 minutes   140 minutes

Ingredients

- 2 pounds of beef stew meat, cut into 1-inch cubes
- 3 tablespoons vegetable oil, divided
- 1 cup water
- 3 large potatoes, peeled and cubed
- 4 carrots, sliced
- 1 large green bell pepper, chopped
- 4 cloves garlic, minced
- 1 onion, chopped
- 2 teaspoons salt
- 1/2 teaspoon ground black pepper
- 1 (14.5 ounces) can of whole peeled tomatoes, chopped
- 2 tablespoons beef bouillon granules
- 1 sugar pumpkin

Pumpkin Stew

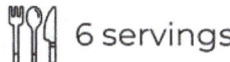 6 servings 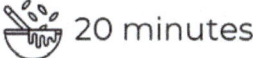 20 minutes 140 minutes

Preparation

- In a large skillet, heat the oil over medium heat (2 teaspoons). In a pot, brown the meat on all sides. In a large bowl, combine the water, potatoes, carrots, green bell pepper, garlic, onion, salt, and pepper. Get the water boiling. Take the heat down and let it simmer for about two hours.
- Add the bouillon to the beef and stir until dissolved. Blend in the canned tomatoes and heat through.
- Put in the 325-degree oven (165 degrees C).
- Remove the pumpkin's pulp and seeds by cutting off the pumpkin's top. Put the pumpkin in a large, deep dish to bake. Put the meat filling in the pumpkin. Spread the leftover oil on the pumpkin's exterior with a brush.
- Put in an oven that has been prepared to 350 degrees for 2 hours. Carve out a dish of pumpkin for each person to enjoy alongside their stew.

Savoury Pumpkin Soup

 6 servings    20 minutes   25 minutes

Ingredients

- 5 cups pumpkin puree
- 2 cups vegetable broth
- 2 cups heavy cream
- 1/2 teaspoon garlic powder
- 1/2 teaspoon onion powder
- 4 ounces of dry pasta
- 1/2 teaspoon pumpkin pie spice
- 1/2 cup fresh parsley, minced
- 1/4 cup cilantro, minced
- 1/4 cup butter, softened
- 1/2 cup plain yoghurt
- 1/2 cup sour cream, for topping
- 1/4 cup shredded mozzarella cheese
- 1/4 cup toasted almonds

Savoury Pumpkin Soup

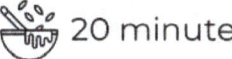 6 servings    20 minutes   25 minutes

Preparation

- Blend the pumpkin, vegetable broth, heavy cream, garlic powder, and onion powder in a large pot. Get the water boiling. Combine the spaghetti with the sauce.
- Pasta should be firm but soft after being cooked for 12 minutes. Put it on low heat and let it simmer.
- Mix in with parsley, cilantro, and pumpkin pie spice. Be careful not to cause any curdling by slowly incorporating the butter, plain yoghurt, and sour cream into the dish.
- Put the cheese in and mix it around so it can melt. Serve with a sprinkle of nuts.

Spiced Turkey Roast

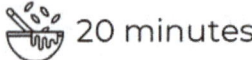 4 servings  20 minutes 130 minutes

Ingredients

- 1 1/2 pounds boneless turkey roast
- 2 teaspoons olive oil
- 2 teaspoons ground cinnamon
- 2 teaspoons ground cloves
- 1 teaspoon ground allspice
- 1 tablespoon coarsely ground black pepper
- 1 cup cranberries

Preparation

- 2 cups water
- 2 tablespoons orange juice
- 1 tablespoon cornstarch
- 2 tablespoons water

Spiced Turkey Roast

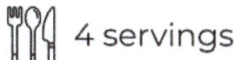 4 servings   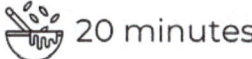 20 minutes    130 minutes

Preparation

- To prepare, set the oven temperature to 350 degrees F. (175 degrees C).
- Rub some olive oil on the turkey and put it in a roasting pan. Mix the ground cinnamon, cloves, allspice, and peppercorns, and rub them all over the turkey.
- The turkey should be roasted for about an hour, or until the juices run clear.
- Make a sauce by bringing 2 cups of water and the cranberries to a boil in a saucepan. Cook on low heat until the cranberries start to pop, then stir in the orange juice. Thicken the sauce by mixing 2 tablespoons of water with the cornstarch or arrowroot. Serve over sliced turkey after cooking until thick.

Spicy Spaghetti Squash

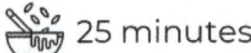 6 servings   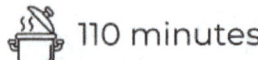 25 minutes   110 minutes

Ingredients

- 1 small spaghetti squash, halved and seeded
- 1 tablespoon olive oil
- 1/2 cup minced onion
- 3 cloves garlic, minced
- 2 green onions, minced
- 12 ounces ground white meat turkey
- 2 cups crushed tomatoes

Preparation

- 2 tablespoons red wine
- 2 teaspoons capers
- 2 teaspoons minced fresh oregano
- 2 teaspoons crushed red pepper flakes
- 2 tablespoons chopped fresh parsley

Spicy Spaghetti Squash

 6 servings  25 minutes 110 minutes

Preparation

- Bake the squash halves, cut side down, in an uncovered baking dish for 45-60 minutes, or until a fork can be inserted into the flesh easily.
- When cool enough to handle, use a big spoon to remove the squash strands and set them aside.
- To prepare, place the oil in a skillet and heat it over medium heat. Stir in the onion, garlic, and scallion and cook for another 2 minutes.
- Put in the turkey and let it cook for 4 minutes.
- Put in the wine and tomatoes, bring to a boil, then reduce the heat and simmer for 20 minutes.
- Mix in the capers, oregano, red pepper flakes, and parsley, and cook at a low simmer for 5 minutes.
- Reheat the squash for 2–3 minutes, covered, in the microwave if it has cooled down. The squash should be served with the sauce on top.

Stuffed Pumpkin I

 4 servings  15 minutes 60 minutes

Ingredients

- 1 cup wild rice
- 1 medium sugar pumpkin
- 2 teaspoons salt
- 1/2 teaspoon dry mustard
- 2 tablespoons bacon grease
- 1 pound ground venison
- 1 onion, chopped
- 3 eggs, beaten
- 1 teaspoon dried sage
- 1/2 teaspoon ground black pepper

Preparation

- To begin, bring 4 cups of water to a boil in a saucepan. Stir in the wild rice. Turn the heat down, cover, and simmer for an hour, or until the meat is soft.
- Set oven temperature to 350 degrees F. (175 degrees C).
- Get rid of the pumpkin's top and use a spoon to dig out the pulp and seeds. Rub 1 teaspoon of salt and dry mustard into the pricked pumpkin interior.
- In a large skillet, melt the bacon fat over medium heat. Combined ground venison and onion should be stirred in. Keep stirring and cooking at a moderate temperature until everything is evenly browned.

Stuffed Pumpkin I

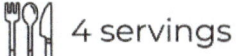 4 servings    15 minutes    60 minutes

Preparation

- Take it away from the heat. Wild rice, the remaining salt, eggs, sage, and pepper should be combined.
- Prepare the venison filling and place it into the pumpkin. Put the pumpkin in a shallow pan and fill it with water by half an inch.
- Put the pumpkin in an oven that has been prepared to 350 degrees Fahrenheit for 1 1/2 hours. If the food is sticking to the pan, add a little extra water.

Apple Strudel II

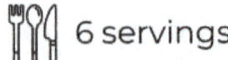 6 servings   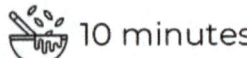 10 minutes   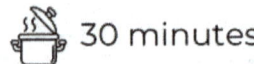 30 minutes

Ingredients

- 3 cups all-purpose flour
- 1 egg, beaten
- 1 cup lukewarm water
- 1 teaspoon white sugar
- 1 teaspoon lard, melted
- 1 pinch salt
- 1 1/2 cups butter, melted
- 1 cup toasted bread crumbs
- 1 cup ground walnuts
- 3 1/2 pounds apples - peeled, cored and thinly sliced
- 3/4 cup raisins
- 1 teaspoon ground cinnamon
- 1 3/4 cups white sugar

Apple Strudel II

 6 servings  10 minutes 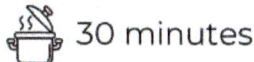 30 minutes

Preparation

- A large bowl should be prepared by sifting all-purpose flour. Egg, water, white sugar, fat, and salt should be combined. Be patient and knead until it's nice and smooth. Spread about a tablespoon's worth of butter and lightly brush. Put a towel over it and wait an hour.
- In a larger bowl, combine the bread crumbs and 3/4 cup of butter. Combine sugar, cinnamon, ground walnuts, apple, and raisins.
- Turn oven temperature up to 375 degrees F. (190 degrees C). Prepare a medium baking dish with a thin layer of butter.
- Stretch and roll the dough into a long, extremely thin rectangle on a large, lightly floured work surface. Thicker parts should be snipped off. Coat with a light coating of melted butter, about half a cup's worth. Leave a two-inch border around the edges of the dough before pressing the breadcrumb mixture in. Strudel is made by rolling out the dough, then folding one end over the filling and rolling it up. Prepared by slicing to suit the baking dish.
- Brush remaining butter over strudel before placing in baking dish. Bake for 1 hour in a preheated oven, until the top is golden and the apples are soft.

Bread Pudding I

 9 servings    10 minutes   90 minutes

Ingredients

- 2 eggs
- 2 egg whites
- 1 1/2 cups skim milk
- 2 tablespoons honey
- 1 teaspoon vanilla extract
- 6 slices raisin bread, cubed

Preparation

- Set oven temperature to 325 degrees F. (165 degrees C). Use nonstick spray to coat one 9-inch pie plate.
- The eggs and egg whites should be mixed in a large bowl and beat until frothy. Whisk in the honey, milk, and vanilla extract.
- Combine the cubed bread and the other ingredients, then pour into a pie dish and stir.
- Allow to bake for 30–35 minutes, or until a knife inserted in the centre comes out clean. Hold back the heat.

Cherry Delight

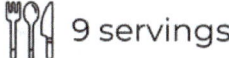 9 servings  25 minutes 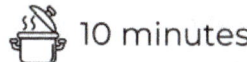 10 minutes

Ingredients

- 6 egg whites
- 2 cups white sugar
- 3/4 teaspoon cream of tartar
- 2 cups crushed saltine crackers
- 1 cup chopped walnuts
- 2 teaspoons vanilla extract
- 2 (21-ounce) cans of cherry pie filling
- 1 (16-ounce) package frozen whipped topping, thawed

Preparation

- To prepare, set the oven temperature to 350 degrees F. (175 degrees C). Prepare a 9x13-inch greased pan.
- Whip the egg whites until they form firm peaks. Beat in sugar and cream of tartar gradually until sugar is dissolved.
- Blend in some crackers, nuts, and vanilla. Pour into the pan and bake at 400 degrees for 25 minutes.
- Take out of the oven, let cool, then divide into squares. Put some whipped cream and pie filling on top of each plate.

Cherry Fluff

16 servings  5 minutes  125 minutes

Ingredients

- 1 (21-ounce) can of cherry pie filling
- 1 (14-ounce) can sweeten condensed milk
- 1 (20-ounce) can crush pineapple, drained
- 1 (8-ounce) container of frozen whipped topping, thawed

Preparation

- Combine cherry pie filling, sweetened condensed milk, crushed pineapple, and whipped topping in a large bowl and set aside.
- Put in the fridge and let it chill for at least 2 hours.

Chocolate Bar Fondue

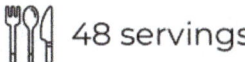 48 servings  5 minutes  15 minutes

Ingredients

- 32 ounces of milk chocolate, grated
- 1 1/4 cups heavy cream
- 1 tablespoon instant coffee powder
- 1 teaspoon vanilla extract
- 1 teaspoon white sugar
- 1/3 cup hot water

Preparation

- For best results, melt the chocolate and cream together in a saucepan over low to medium heat.
- Stir in the sugar, vanilla extract, boiling water, and instant coffee.
- Stirring constantly, keep heating the mixture over low heat until it is completely smooth.

Country Banana Bread

🍴 12 servings  15 minutes  1hr minutes

Ingredients

- 1 (18.25 ounce) package of yellow cake mix
- 3 eggs
- 1 1/3 cups vegetable oil
- 4 bananas, mashed

Preparation

- To prepare, set the oven temperature to 350 degrees F. (175 degrees C). Prepare a 9x13-inch greased pan.
- Cake mix, eggs, oil, and bananas should all be combined in one basin. Put the contents of the bowl into the pan.
- Cook for 35-40 minutes in an oven warmed to 350 degrees Fahrenheit (175 degrees Celsius).

Corn Pudding II

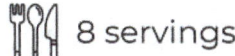 8 servings  20 minutes  45 minutes

Ingredients

- 2 (10-ounce) packages of frozen corn kernels, thawed
- 6 eggs
- 3 1/2 cups milk
- 1/2 cup butter, melted
- 4 tablespoons all-purpose flour
- 1 cup white sugar

Preparation

- To prepare, set the oven temperature to 350 degrees F. (175 degrees C).
- Eggs should be thoroughly mixed in a blender or food processor. Flour and sugar should be added and mixed thoroughly. Blend the milk in a little bit. Lastly, incorporate the corn by hand. Add the melted butter and mix well before pouring it into a large casserole dish.
- Bake for 45 minutes at 350 degrees F (175 degrees C). When the pudding is ready, it will have a firm middle and a lovely golden brown colour on top. Ideally, you'd wait around 15 minutes before serving it warm.

Apple Cranberry Streusel Pie

🍴 10 servings　🥣 120 minutes　🍲 65 minutes

Ingredients

- Pastry for a single-crust 9-inch pie
- 1 cup Equal® Spoonful*
- 1 tablespoon cornstarch
- 1 1/2 cups fresh or frozen, thawed cranberries
- 1 cup apple cider or unsweetened apple juice
- 1/4 cup Equal® Spoonful**
- 3/4 teaspoon ground cinnamon
- 1/4 teaspoon ground nutmeg
- 1/4 teaspoon salt
- 5 cups sliced, cored, peeled Granny Smith or other baking apples
- Streusel Topping:
- 1/4 cup quick or old-fashioned oats, uncooked
- 3 tablespoons all-purpose flour
- 1/2 cup Equal® Spoonful***
- 1 teaspoon ground cinnamon
- 1/2 teaspoon ground nutmeg
- 4 tablespoons cold stick butter or margarine, cut into pieces

Apple Cranberry Streusel Pie

10 servings  25 minutes  85 minutes

Preparation

- A 9-inch pie pan should be inverted onto a floured surface, and the pastry should be rolled into a circle that is 1 inch bigger than the pan.
- Gently press the pastry into the prepared pan.
- Stir in the cranberries and apple cider to the cornstarch and Equal® Spoonful* that has been combined with 1 cup of water in a small pot. Bring to a boil, then decrease the heat to low and cook for approximately a minute while stirring frequently, or until thickened.
- Toss apples in a large basin with a mixture of 1/4 cup Equal® Spoonful**, cinnamon, nutmeg, and salt. Add the cranberry sauce to the apples and stir to combine. Spread Streusel Topping over fruit and arrange in pie crust.
- In a small bowl, mix the oats, flour, 1/2 cup Equal® Spoonful***, cinnamon, and nutmeg for the Streusel Topping. Then, using a pastry blender, cut in the butter until the mixture resembles coarse crumbs. In a pie, this is the finishing touch.
- In a preheated oven at 400 degrees Fahrenheit, bake the pie for 50-60 minutes, or until the pastry is brown and the apples are soft. If you want to keep your pie from getting too brown in the oven, cover it with a loose sheet of aluminium foil for the last 20 to 30 minutes of baking. Set the wire rack in the refrigerator to cool. Hold back the heat.

www.ingramcontent.com/pod-product-compliance
Lightning Source LLC
Chambersburg PA
CBHW081709100526
44590CB00022B/3711